Arab-Islamic Philosophy
A CONTEMPORARY CRITIQUE

Middle East Monograph Series
No. 12

Arab-Islamic Philosophy
A CONTEMPORARY CRITIQUE

by

Mohammed 'Abed al-Jabri

١١١

Translated from the French
by Aziz Abbassi

The Center for Middle Eastern Studies
The University of Texas at Austin

Library of Congress Catalogue Card Number: 99-070635
ISBN: 0-292-70480-1

Printed in the United States of America

Cover photograph of Tinmal (twelfth-century mosque in the Atlas Mountains
of Morocco) taken by Ron Baker

Cover design: Diane Watts

Editor: Annes McCann-Baker

Published in French as *introduction à la critique de la raison arabe*
by éditions la découverte/institut du monde arabe 1994

The Center gratefully acknowledges the Institute for Maghrebi Studies (AIMS)
for a research grant that helped with the translation of this book.

Table of Contents

Introduction by Walid Hamarneh   vii

Author's Introduction   1

PART ONE
A DIFFERENT READING OF THE TRADITION DISCOURSE

CHAPTER I
The Present Shortcomings   9

CHAPTER II
For a Scientific Critique of Arab Reason   16

PART TWO
PHILOSOPHICAL THINKING AND IDEOLOGY

CHAPTER III
Historical Dynamics of the Arab-Islamic Philosophy   47

CHAPTER IV
The Rise and Fall of Reason   55

CHAPTER V
The Andalusian Resurgence   63

CONCLUSION
The Future Can Only Be Averroist   120

Introduction
by
Walid Hamarneh

This introductory collection of essays by Mohammed 'Abed al-Jabri is the first of his works to appear in the English language. The fact that very little is known about him in North America may seem rather strange, as his writings and ideas have been at the center of academic debates in the Arab world since the mid 1970s.[1] This situation being so, my main objective is to provide the reader with some background on Jabri's life and work, to summarize the intellectual and cultural context within which his work is seen as a new and fresh challenge, and to point out some of his ideas and hypotheses that are not represented in the following essays. I will, therefore, try to complement the essays here rather than only summarize them. In doing so, my emphasis will be on certain aspects of his work that I think are crucial for researchers, scholars, and academics who are interested in Islam, the Middle East and the Arab world.

Mohammed 'Abed al-Jabri was born 1936 in Figuig in south-eastern Morocco. He was brought up in a family that supported the Istiqlal Party (a party that lead the struggle for independence and unity of Morocco when it was under French and Spanish occupation). He was sent first to a religious school, then to a private nationalist school *(madrasah hurrah wataniyah)*, which was founded by the Independence movement. From 1951-53 he spent two years at a government high school in Casablanca. Following Morocco's independence, al-Jabri earned the Arabic High School Diploma (Science Section).

Mehdi Ben Barka (who lead the leftists in the Istiqlal party and later split from it to found in 1959 the Union Nationale des Forces Populaires (UNFP) [later Union Socialiste des Forces Populaires (USFP)], guided the youthful al-Jabri. He prompted him to begin working for al-'Alam, which was then the official publication of the Istiqlal Party. In 1958 al-Jabri started studying philosophy at the University of Damascus in Syria, but left one year later to join the newly founded University of Rabat. His political activities never ceased, and in July 1963 he was incarcerated, like many of his comrades in the UNFP, under the pretext of conspiring against the state.

From 1964 al-Jabri taught philosophy at the high-school level and was active in the sphere of educational evaluation and planning. In 1966 he published jointly with Mustafa al-'Omari and Ahmed as-Sattati two textbooks designed for the final year of high school. One was on Islamic thought[2] and the other on philosophy.[3] The latter book had a great impact on students during the late sixties and early seventies; it emphasized the relationship between culture and society, and the importance the role education and knowledge play in changing society.[4] As a result of his activities in the educational sphere, problems of education constituted a fairly important part of his intellectual production during that period; every few years al-Jabri published articles on issues and problems of education, especially those found in Morocco.[5]

After completing his state examination in 1967 (his unpublished thesis was entitled *Falsafat al-tarikh 'inda Ibn Khaldun*, "The Philosophy of History of Ibn Khaldun," under the supervision of M. Aziz Lahbabi), he started teaching philosophy at the University of Mohammed V in Rabat. In 1970 he completed his Ph.D. (Doctorat d'Etat) with a thesis on the thought of Ibn Khaldun under the supervision of Najib Baladi.[6] During the seventies al-Jabri began publishing a series of papers on Islamic thought that immediately drew the attention of many intellectuals and academics in the Arab World, including for the first time those in the Levant. He also published in 1976 two volumes on epistemology (one on mathematics and modern rationalism, the second on the empirical method and the development of scientific thought). However, most of his energies were then still dedicated to political work, and in 1975 he became a member of the political bureau of the USFP, of which he was one of the founders. By the early eighties, however, he felt he had to concentrate his energies on his intellectual and scholarly work and quit his position in the party's political bureau (though not his other activities) in 1981 to concentrate on writing. In 1980, he had collected and published a number of papers written earlier and presented in conferences on Islamic philosophers. The title of this volume is *Nahnu wa al-turath*, which can be loosely translated as "our heritage and us." Two years later he published a book on contemporary Arab thought, *al-Khitab al-'Arabi al-mu'asir: Dirasah tahliliyah naqdiyah* (Contemporary Arab Discourse: A Critical and Analytical Study). This was followed by his three-volume magnum opus entitled *Naqd al-'aql al-'Arabi* (Critique of Arab Reason) published in 1984, 1986, and 1990.

Aziz Abbassi's English translation in the following pages is from the French *Introduction à la critique de la raison Arabe*, translated from Arabic to French by Ahmed Mahfoud and Marc Geoffroy, published by La Dècouverte in 1994. The occasion of this French publication was an effort to provide an introduction to al-Jabri's thought prior to publication of a translation of his three-volume *Naqd al-'aql al-'Arabi,* referred to earlier. The essays were selected from al-Jabri's earlier work, especially his collection *Nahnu wa al-turath*. The author advised in the selection of the texts and revised the French edition, thus making it authoritative. And, although the present text was translated from the French, it was compared with the Arabic original.

During the past few years, al-Jabri has published essays and shorter monographs on issues ranging from democracy and human rights in the Arab world to further elaboration and discussions of his main theses in his previously published work. Al-Jabri's work is a direct and critical intervention in problems and issues that are central to modern and contemporary Arab thought. Because his interpretations and readings of modern and classical Arab thought in more than one instance challenge that thought, I will not only sum-marize some of his ideas but also discuss briefly some of the main trends of intellectual discussions in the Arab world during the past few decades.

Arab thought, since the middle of the nineteenth century (a pe-riod generally called the Renaissance [*nahdah*]), has been dominated by acknowledgment of the inferiority of the Arab and Islamic world of the present, when seen in contradistinction to that of the modern West and the classical "golden" period of the Arab-Islamic Empire. Thinkers and intellectuals were torn between the seduction of West-ern thought with its superiority in the economic, scientific, techno-logical, and military spheres, while being attracted to the Arab past, since it provided proof that Arabs and Muslims are also capable of holding a leading position in world culture and learning. It also pro-vided reassurance that Arabs still held the upper ground in religion, literature and social ethics. Reactions and proposed solutions to this diverged, but all were implicated in this tension between the two intellectual traditions.[7]

The basic problem was how to catch up and rebuild Arab thought while preserving its identity and authenticity. There were, of course, those voices that advocated a return to the values of the early past, which was, according to them, the only way for Arabs and Muslims to regain their place in the world. There were also a few voices that proposed becoming a part of the modern world by completely shed-ding the past. However, most voices and movements advocated one type or another of eclecticism that combined what was seen as posi-tive in both of the two models.

Following the second world war and the political independence of many Arab states, coupled with the rise of radical brands of na-tionalism, socialism, and Islamism, the discourse of the *nahdah* was conceived as having been too reformist and as having over-empha-sized aspects of culture and education. A new "revolutionary" dis-course developed, especially during the fifties and the sixties, that emphasized the political and the economic, and laid more emphasis on the voluntarist revolutionary ideologies of transforming societies. Despite these differences, both the "reformist" and the "revolutionary" discourses were implicated within the same old problematic of catching up while preserving authenticity. The central aspect of these issues relevant to our purpose here is that the past was always part of the argument and determined in many ways the parameters for what was conceived of as authenticity.

With the Arab defeat in 1967, intellectual discussions began to change rather quickly. And although the more radical revolutionary discourses assumed central stage during the immediate aftermath of the war, it was a resuscitated Islamic discourse (in both its "conservative" and "revolutionary" brands) that gradually set the parameters for explaining the Arab defeat and the collapse of attempts at modernization. This does not mean that Islamist discourse reigned supreme. To the contrary, it was still a minority view among the educated elite and intellectuals. But, starting with the late sixties, at the center of most discussions was the issue of the Arab-Islamic past. Or to put it differently, there was a shift from discussing the problems of the present, as such, to discussing them as extensions of the past. But, as the past is always being constructed in ways that are implicated with the present, the intellectual battles shifted from being interpretations of the present to interpretations of the past.

Radical (including Marxist), as well as other modernizing discourses positioned themselves as agenda for the future. These agendas were formulated to show that they were extensions of age-old dimensions that go back to the early stages of the development of Islam, have indigenous roots, and are therefore authentic. "Liberal" modernizing trends emphasized that Islam promoted values like hard work and private property, or emphasized rational tendencies in Islamic thought (both philosophical and religious), or emphasized Islamic democratic practices that were re-interpreted to look like modern democratic ones.[8] Many leftists, on the other hand saw their own ideological and political roots in social and revolutionary movements in Islam, or tried to find since the earliest stages in the history of Islam a left and a right that represented well defined class interests.[9] There were also pioneering attempts by some Marxists (like the Lebanese Husayn Muruwwah and the Syrian al-Tayyib Tizini) to interpret and explain trends in Islamic thought and philosophy by relating them to social and political roots.[10]

The past (read as constructed tradition and heritage)[11] was seen to be the legitimizing basis for the ideas of the present, and the traditionalists fought the ideological battles of the present in what was considered their own historic turf, and gradually set the parameters of the ideological discourse and dominated it. This, I should emphasize, was not due to their presenting the most potent or convincing arguments and interpretations, but rather to having forced others to grant a conception of legitimacy that was their own. After all, it was traditionalists who had been constructing tradition and heritage in the Arab-Islamic area for at least the past nine centuries. The Arab World and especially its cultural institutions became more and more dependent upon money pumped into those institutions by conservative Arab oil-producing countries. It was in those countries' interests to promote ideological constructs based upon Islam and Islamic discourse rather than secular (nationalist, liberal, or Marxist) discourse. These governments, after all, had spent most of the previous decades fighting "revolutionary" nationalisms (like the Ba'th Party and Nasserism) as well as Communism in the Arab World.

It is within such an intellectual climate that al-Jabri made his contributions. His criticism is directed at the three trends mentioned earlier: the traditionalist, the liberal (which includes the orientalist tradition), and the orthodox Marxist. His earlier works had emphasized three-dimensional readings of the Arab past as alternatives. By this he means that he reads texts structurally, historically and ideologically. His justification lies in that he sees thought being determined by two things: the field of knowledge (*al-haql al-ma'rifi*) and the ideological content (*al-madmun al-idyuluji*). The first implies the field in which thought moves, which is composed of material of knowledge (*maddah ma'rifiyah*) and a thinking apparatus (*jihaz tafkiri*). The second implies the possible social and political functions of that thought. Such a reading, according to al-Jabri, provides an alternative to those other readings that emphasized either the material of knowledge or the ideological content. Al-Jabri also starts from the premise that, due to the development of knowledge and especially the sciences since medieval times, the substantive knowledge in classical Arab-Islamic philosophical and scientific thought is useless from our perspective. Emphasis should be given to the thinking apparatuses, but within the context of ways the material of knowledge was treated. This means that although the material of knowledge is useless for us today, it is nevertheless relevant to any intellectual enterprise that attempts to understand classical Arab-Islamic thought.

The second aspect in these essays that needs to be highlighted is that although these were separate essays written on different occasions, they are connected by a thread of thought.[12] This hypothesis disagrees with a consensus among almost all (orientalists, traditionalists, liberals, and Marxists) who have studied classical Arab-Islamic philosophy. This consensus is that Muslim philosophers have operated within an Aristotelian paradigm (or at least a paradigm that followed the late Hellenistic interpretations of Aristotle, tainted with some Neo-Platonism mainly derived from the false ascription of the *Enneads* of Plotinus to Aristotle). Accordingly, though there are some differences as to the extent to which the Muslim thinkers conformed to (and even understood) Greek thought, especially that of Aristotle, they are seen as a chain of transmitters and commentators on Greek philosophy.

Al-Jabri developed a new hypothesis in which he maintained that there was not such a chain, nor was there such a continuity among all these philosophers. To the contrary, there was an epistemological break[13] between the philosophers of the East (the eastern parts of the Islamic Empire) and those of the West (Andalusia and Morocco). This epistemological break can be seen not only in the writings of philosophers, but also in the writings of jurists and legal scholars (such as Ibn Hazm), as well as theologians (such as al-Shatibi), and very prominently in the writings of Ibn Khaldun. In conjunction with this, al-Jabri provided a controversial and unorthodox interpretation of Ibn Sina as not being the best representative of Islamic rationalism in the East, but as being a thinker who consecrated irrationalism not only in his texts on Eastern philosophy, but also in his philosophical legacy. According to this interpretation, both Ibn Sina and al-Ghazali (considered to be opposing intellectual figures by most historians of Islamic thought) are seen as a part of the same philosophical problematic. They disagreed about solutions to certain problems within it but, nonetheless, shared it, along with al-Farabi and most other Eastern thinkers.[14]

These and similar ideas were later developed in al-Jabri's three-volume *Naqd al-'aql al-'Arabi* (Critique of Arab Reason). Since this work represents the most developed form of the thinking of al-Jabri, which is seen in its early conceptions in the following translation, it is instructive to look at the ideas in *Naqd al-'aql al-'Arabi* in some detail. In the first volume, he developed the basic concepts to be used in his analysis and emphasized that the purpose of his study was not the ideological content of Arab-Islamic thought, nor its substantive content, as much as the epistemological systems present in it. He then developed another concept (well represented in this translation) that the frame of reference for early Arab thought is neither the pre-Islamic period nor the era of Muhammad and the first four Caliphs, but is rather the age of "codification," or recording (asr al-tadwin), during the second hijra century (eighth century). He followed with a genealogy of the main ideas present in Arab thought in the classical period and concluded that there are three epistemological systems represented. He called them the system of indication, or explication (*bayan*), the system of illumination or gnosticism (*'irfan*), and the system of demonstration or inferential evidence (*burhan*). By epistemological system, al-Jabri means something that is similar to Foucault's *episteme*, and not just merely procedural rules or protocols of research.

The second volume in the Critique is dedicated to the analysis of these three epistemological systems. The analysis develops their basic characteristics and concepts, and then follows with an analysis of examples, taken mostly from texts that have assumed a classical position within Arab thought.

For al-Jabri, the epistemological system of Indication or Explication is historically the earliest within Arab thought. It became dominant in the so-called indigenous sciences: philology, jurisprudence and legal sciences (*fiqh*), Qur'anic sciences (interpretations, hermeneutics and exegesis), dialectical theology (*kalam*), and non-philosophical literary theory. It started out being a combination of rules for interpreting discourse and determining the conditions of discourse production.[15] Its fundamental concepts combined the methods of *fiqh* as developed by al-Shafi'i with that of rhetoric as developed by al-Jahiz. It was centered on the relationship between utterance and meaning, in addition to which later jurists and theologians have added conditions of certainty, analogy, subject matter of the report, and levels of authenticity or reliability.

The overall result was a theory of knowledge that was explicatory (*bayani*) at all levels. At the level of its internal logic, that theory of knowledge was governed by the concept of indication, which implied elocution, enunciation, understanding, communication, and reception. This is true also at the level of the material of knowledge, composed mainly of the Qur'an, the hadith, grammar, *fiqh*, and Arabic poetry and prose; and true also at the ideological level, since the determining authoritative force behind this level had been Islamic dogma, and was therefore restricted from the beginning to equating knowledge with belief in God. It also applied at the epistemological level, where humans are conceived as being endowed with the capacity of *bayan,* which is grounded in two types of "reason": one innate, the other acquired.

The type of reason that is innate is God-given. That which is acquired is through report and cogitation as determined by the authenticity of transmission, whereas cogitation involves thinking not about reason as much as about the proof that lies outside or beyond the boundaries of reason. Reason's function is to examine the world as manifestations or signs of that which is there, but cannot directly be perceived. This is according to the rules of reasoning, by analogy of the unknown after the known (*qiyas al-gha'ib 'ala al-shahid*), which is explained in the essays that follow..

Al-Jabri proceeded to uncover the basis of the *bayan* mode of reasoning and showed how it operated in Islamic law, in grammatical and philological studies, and in theology (*kalam*). He concluded that the system of Indication is governed by the two principles of discontinuity, or separation (*infisal*), and contingency, or possibility (*tajwiz*). These principles are manifest in the theory of individual substance (*al-jawhar al-fard*), which maintains that the relationship between individual substances (bodies, actions, sensations, and everything the world is made up of) is one based upon contiguity and association, but not influence and interaction. This theory leaves no place for a theory of causality or for the idea of a (natural) law.

Al-Jabri posited that the origins of such an epistemological system lay in a misconstrued idea of the Bedouin (*Arabi*): the sole referential authority was not simply to the Qur'an, but also to its reading through the world view of the pre-Islamic nomadic Arab (the vehicle of which was the pre-Islamic Arabic language). That language became the sole arbiter and frame of reference, because it was seen as the language of the Qur'an. This, according to al-Jabri, is a construct that was made during the age of codification and which was used as a legitimating principle.

Illumination, or gnosticism, for al-Jabri originated in Eastern and hermetical thought and is based upon what is termed "inner revelation and insight" as an epistemological method. These practices include Sufism, Shi`i thought, Isma`ili philosophy, oriental philosophy of illumination, theosophy, magic, astrology, alchemy, and esoteric and Sufi Qur'anic exegesis. Gnostic epistemological systems are based upon the dichotomy of the obvious or manifest (*zahir*) and esoteric or latent (*batin*). The latent is accorded a higher status in the hierarchy of gnostic knowledge. Gnostic analogy (*mumathalah*) is different from both explicatory analogy (*qiyas bayani*) and from logical syllogism because it is based upon direct similarities. But, since gnostic analogy is based upon similarity, it is not rule-bound and can acquire an infinite number of forms and levels: it can take the form of a simile or a figure of speech; it can be a representation, but it can also be borrowed from the analogy of the unknown after the known; and it can also be based upon correspondence. But al-Jabri argues that there were basically three types of such analogies in gnostic epistemology: similarity based upon numerical correspondence, similarity based upon representation, and rhetorical and poetic similarity. Al-Jabri saw that this epistemological system had been productive in literature and the arts, but as a rationalist, he saw no value to it in matters of reason. To the contrary he called it "resigned reason" (*al-'aql al-mustaqil*).

The epistemological system of demonstration, based on inferential evidence, al-Jabri saw as having its origins in Greek thought (especially Aristotle), but he did not restrict it to those who had based their analysis on logic. His concept of demonstration is much wider and encompasses the rationality of Ibn Rushd, the critical attitude of Ibn Hazm, the historicism of Ibn Khaldun and the fundamental theology of al-Shatibi. In contradistinction to *bayan*, which develops its understanding of the world on the principles of discontinuity and contingency, and gnosis, which bases its understanding on the principles of correspondence and similarity, the epistemological system of Demonstration is based upon the causal connections between elements, thereby making the idea of a (natural) law possible. Since al-Jabri equates this with rationalism, which is generally well-known, I will not spend more time discussing it, but will move towards the last two points to be highlighted in this introduction.

Al-Jabri developed a hypothesis that the Demonstrative epistemological system was used in many cases in the service of the two other epistemic systems. A case in point is Ibn Sina, who utilized inferential evidence to serve his fundamentally gnostic philosophy. Al-Jabri maintained that this was essentially the destiny of the system of demonstration in the East (again implying the eastern parts of the Islamic Empire), but was generally not the case in the West (Andalusia and Morocco), thereby emphasizing the earlier hypothesis of an epistemological break between the two.

Another point to be emphasized is that al-Jabri did not see these three epistemological systems present in ideal forms in the thought of any individual thinker. Each is always present in a more-or-less contaminated form. However, he differentiated between having elements of one system present as a minor part within a dominant system in the thought of a specific thinker (Ibn Rushd is basically a proponent of the system of demonstration), and two systems (or even three) present in the work of some thinkers. To return to one of his earlier hypothesis that Ibn Sina and al-Ghazali belong to the same problematic, he emphasized that both thinkers were hybrid, in the sense that in their work one can see the epistemological systems of demonstration and illumination. What is also interesting is that, despite many of the points in which they disagreed, both, according to al-Jabri, opted for using the system of demonstration (rationalism) in the service of the system of illumination.

In the third volume of *Naqd al-ʿaql al-Arabi*, entitled "Arab Political Reason," al-Jabri shifts his focus from uncovering the epistemological systems governing Arab thought to those governing thinking about reality. He, therefore, does not resort to his earlier classification based upon the three epistemological systems, but introduces new concepts that fit his different subject matter. Utilizing a number of concepts from the modern French *imaginaire sociale* (social imaginary) in conjunction with concepts derived from classical Arab thought, he develops his ideas around three concepts: the tribe (*qabilah*), plunder (*al-ghanimah*), and dogma (*al-ʿaqidah*). He then studies the manifestations of these conceptual frameworks, especially during the latter stages of the development of the Islamic polity.

I hope that this brief and overly simplified summary has given the reader a taste of the depth of the ideas and hypotheses of al-Jabri. I think one has to reiterate here that in addition to these general theoretical hypotheses, al-Jabri is at his best when he analyzes texts—not only texts that are relatively unknown but, most importantly, texts that have been analyzed many times by competent scholars. What he does with these texts is discover something new and interesting. This is due not only to his method of textual analysis, nor his knowledge, but also to the fact that he does not approach texts as instances of institutionalized knowledge as much as he attempts to reconstruct them from a new conceptual perspective. A text by a grammarian, or one by a legal scholar or a theologian, turns in his hand into a fresh and "new" text. The chapters that follow represent al-Jabri's own introduction to his major interventions in this regard.

---

[1] There is a short summary of some of Jabri's ideas in 'Issa Boullata's book: *Trends and Issues in Contemporary Arab Thought*. Albany: SUNY Press, 1990, pp. 45-55. See also a different kind of exposition of his ideas with a special emphasis on his reading of Averroes in Anke von Kugelgen: *Averroes und die arabische Moderne: Ansatze zu einer Neubegrundung des Rationalismus in Islam*. Leiden: E.J. Brill, 1994, pp. 260-288.

[2] *Al-Fikr al-Islami li-tullab al-Bakaluriya*. Al-Dar al-Bayda': Dar al-Nashr al-Maghribiyah, 1966. Many later printings of this book were made.

[3] *Durus fi al-falsafah li-tullab al-Bakaluriya*. Al-Dar al-Bayda': Dar al-Nashr al-Maghribiyah, 1966. Many later printings of this book were made.

[4] See M.A. al-Jabri: "Masar katib" in: *al-Karmel* 11 (1984), p. 162, and the roundtable discussion under the title "Naqd al-'aql al-'Arabi fi mashru al-Jabri" in: *al-Wahdah*, vol. III, 26-27 (October/November 1986, pp. 135-165).

[5] His book *Min ajl ru'yah taqaddumiyah li-ba'd mushkilatina al-fikriyah wa-al-tarbawiyah.* Al-Dar al-Bayda': Dar al-Nashr al-Maghribiyah, 1977, includes some of these essays. He published articles in *al-Aqlam* on education in Morocco, as well as some in the daily *al-Sharq al-Awsat.*

[6] This thesis was published as *Fikr Ibn Khaldun: al-'Asabiyah wa-al-dawlah: Ma'alim nazariyah khalduniyah fi al-tarikh al-Islami.* Al-Dar al-Bayda': Dar al-Thaqafah, 1971. This book was later published in Lebanon and went through a number of printings.

[7] For a fine survey of Arab thought during this period, see Albert Hourani's *Arabic Thought in the Liberal Age 1798-1939.*: Cambridge University Press, 1983.

[8] The most prominent of these was the thought of Zaki Najib Mahmu, who was until the sixties the most prominent logical positivist in the Arab World who had completely rejected classical Arab-Islamic thought as completely irrelevant to our modern times, but then turned his attention to it and produced a number of books showing his change of mind by emphasizing what he saw as the rationalist trends in Islamic thought.

[9] It is worth noting here that many books were published during the late sixties and early seventies with titles like "the left and right in Islam" or series of books on the Qur'an, Muhammad, and the caliphs Abu Bakr, 'Umar, and 'Ali reinterpreted from a rather mechanical and naïve right/left dichotomy that was seen as reflecting a class struggle between the poor classes and the rich classes. I have to emphasize a number of points in this respect. First, there were a number of Marxists who did not accept these simplistic interpretations of Islamic history. Second, that these interpretations were not new but were basically developed by historians like Bandali al-Jawzi (a Palestinian who studied and taught in the Soviet Union during the thirties and forties) and depended mostly on the writings of orientalists. Third, that with the rise of religious minorities in the political leadership of some Arab countries and some "leftist" political parties, such interpretations were welcome as they tended to justify the "revolutionary" traditions of these same minorities or their historical antecedents.

[10] Works by these authors were criticized by many scholars including Marxists like Nayif Balluz and Tawfiq Sallum. Muruwwah and Tizini were taken to task because both resorted to what was seen as a simplistic materialism/idealism dichotomy which was dominant in soviet Marxism, and for resorting to a rather crude interpretation of the socio-economic history of the Islamic Empire. Tizini, who teaches philosophy at the University of Damascus, studied with the (then) East German

philosophy Professor Hermann Ley, while the work of Muruwwah was originally his doctoral dissertation prepared in the Soviet Union. Both, but especially Tizini, had some influence on the work of al-Jabri.

[11] The Arabic word "turath" is a loaded term both semantically and ideologically. I have not been able to find a word in English that conveys the sense of the word in Arabic. I have, therefore, resorted to the words "tradition and heritage" as a pair.

[12] This thread of thought is embodied in all al-Jabri's readings, whether it is the political philosophy of al-Farabi, or the re-interpretation of Ibn Sina, or the reading of the philosophers of North Africa and the Andalus (especially Ibn Tufayl, Ibn Bajah, and Ibn Rushd) as rationalists who have broken with the philosophical paradigms of the eastern parts of the Islamic world.

[13] Al-Jabri borrows the (by now very popular) term from the French philosopher Gaston Bachelard.

[14] This hypothesis is developed in al-Jabri's papers on al-Farabi and Ibn Sina in his book *Nahnu wa al-turath* pp. 55-166.

[15] Al-Jabri here disagrees with an idea advocated by most orientalists and many Arabs, including Taha Husayn, that the shift within indigenous sciences from the emphasis on the conditions of discourse production to one on rules of interpretation was the result of the influence of Greek thought and logic. He maintains that it was actually due to the development of *'ilm usul al-fiqh* (principles of jurisprudence). He also goes into detail showing the many differences between the Greek (read Aristotelian) logical *qiyas* (syllogism) and the *qiyas* (analogy) of the jurists and grammarians.

Author's Introduction

To Seek Our Modernity by Rethinking Our Tradition (*turath*)

Voices are clamoring here and there to question, in one way or another, the Arab researchers' concern over tradition: why all the interest in tradition? Is this not an intellectual regression? Some even go as far as referring to a pathological phenomenon, a "collective neurosis" that suddenly hit Arab intellectuals following the 1967 debacle, and caused them to turn backwards in the direction of "tradition." Those who hold such an opinion raise the objection that the interest in the topic of "tradition" diverts minds from the exigencies of modernity. Under their delusion, they believe that the Arab-Islamic tradition, and for that matter any other tradition, is nothing but an object from the past that should be conveniently relegated into the past, and its study carefully reserved—if ever deemed useful—for the sole care of those rare scholars who specialize in things of the past. Interest in tradition should in this case remain cloistered within the walls of academic institutions or the pages of specialized journals. In other words, the "superfluous" interest in tradition of Arab intellectuals would inevitably express itself at the expense of their interest in "modernity."

But I believe that this point of view does not sufficiently take into account the specificity of those problems posited within Arab culture. Indeed, what makes the latter quite distinct, from the time of "codification," or recording, (*'asr al-tadwin*)[1] to the present time, is the fact that its internal dynamics does not express itself in the production of new discursive forms but rather in the reproduction

1

of the old. Beginning in the seventeenth century of the hijra, this reproductive activity was interrupted, giving way to a state of inertia, of withdrawal and of repetition. Since then, a certain notion of—what I have called—"an understanding of tradition confined within tradition" settled into the Arab-Islamic culture and is prevalent to this day. Under these conditions, modernity would perhaps consist in going beyond this understanding of tradition that is confined within tradition, in order to establish a modern understanding and a contemporary view of tradition. Modernity, therefore, is not to refute tradition or break with the past, but rather to upgrade the manner in which we assume our relationship to tradition at the level of what we call "contemporaneity," which, for us, means catching up with the great strides that are being made worldwide. True, modernity must find the substantiation of its theses within its own discourse, the discourse of contemporaneity, but must not be a "fundamentalism" that clings to some inspiring sources/foundations. Alas, modernity in contemporary Arab thought has not gone that far yet. It remains limited—in the conception of its theses—to getting its inspiration from European modernity, from which it draws the rationale and the "foundations" to its discourse. Now, even if we admit that European modernity currently represents "universal" modernity, its very membership within the specific cultural history of Europe—even as a figure of opposition—makes European modernity incapable of analyzing Arab cultural reality, whose history was shaped far away from it. European modernity is foreign to Arab culture and to its history and could not possibly establish a dialogue that is likely to trigger a movement in its midst. Since European modernity can only engage Arab culture from the outside, it thus pushes its adversary into withdrawal and confinement. This is why our aspiration toward modernity must by necessity base itself on those components of the critical mind that are present within the Arab culture itself, in order to trigger an internal dynamics of change. Modernity, therefore, means first and foremost to develop a modern method and a modern vision of tradition.

We could thus rid our conception of tradition from that ideological and emotional charge that weighs on our conscience and forces us to perceive tradition as an absolute reality that transcends history, instead of perceiving it in its relativity and its historicity.

What is going to ensure the specificity of our modernity will therefore be that part which it will play within contemporary Arab culture. It is indeed its ability to fulfill this part which will make of it a truly "Arab modernity." In fact, there is not *one* single absolute, universal and planetary modernity; rather, there are *numerous* modernities that differ from era to era and from place to place. In other words, modernity is an historical phenomenon, and as such, it remains conditioned by the circumstances within which it manifests itself, and confined within the space-time limitations defined by its *becoming* throughout history. Modernity must therefore differ according to each space and each historical experience, e.g., European modernity is different from either Chinese modernity or Japanese modernity. If in Europe they have come to speak of post-modernism, it is because the very phenomenon of modernity had ceased by the end of the nineteenth century. Modernity was an historical stage born of the Age of Enlightenment (the eighteenth century), which was itself born following the Renaissance (the sixteenth century).

The situation in the Arab world is quite different. Here, the Renaissance, the Age of Enlightenment and modernity are not successive periods that surpass one another; rather, they are intertwined and coexist well within the contemporary era whose beginnings go back about one hundred years. When we speak of modernity, we must not therefore understand it as do the European intellectuals and researchers for whom modernity is a stage that represents the transcending of the Age of Enlightenment and of the Renaissance, the latter having in fact flourished thanks to the "resurrection" of the "tradition" of Antiquity and thanks to a particular way of subscribing to this tradition. Modernity, as it manifests itself in our present situation, is at the same time the Renaissance, the Age of

Enlightenment and the *transcending* of these two periods. All expressions of modernity will have to be centered around rationality and democracy. These two principles are not merely borrowed objects but concrete practices that answer to specific rules. As long as we have not applied rationality to our own tradition, exposed the sources and denounced the manifestations of despotism in this tradition, we will most assuredly remain incapable of building a modernity of our own through which we can engage in the "universal" modernity, no longer as patients but as agents.

A number of people who extol modernity may object that, as far as they are concerned, "universal modernity" as such is like a presence that derives its norms from itself. Though I doubt very much that such a situation, i.e., that of an intellectual who would live a modernity that would only derive its norms from within itself—is even possible, we would conceivably allow such a thesis if the question was only to resolve individual problems. Speaking in this fashion, this intellectual is thinking according to his own criteria and is narrowing down the problem to the data of his personal experience. Some might judge this position to be in effect a modernist one in so far as modernity consecrates individuality as a value in itself, that modernity is "individualistic." Unfortunately, this is a false conception of modernity, for if it were the case, these intellectuals would not even feel the need to criticize the interest of others in tradition. They would have no need for the "other" if modernity were in fact purely individualistic.

In fact, modernity can be an individual position only in as far as it is tied to a rise of the critical mind and of creativity within a given culture and in so far as these two activities are performed by individuals as such and not as representatives of the group. By the same token, modernity is not a negative attitude, nor is it an attitude of withdrawal and retirement within oneself. Despite the status it confers on the individual as a value in and of itself, modernity is therefore not an end in itself. It happens of necessity for the sake of someone other than the self and in view of all the phenomena of the culture from which it has emerged. Modernity for the sake of modernity is an absurd idea. Modernity is a message and an impetus of change aimed at reviving mentalities, the norms of thinking and of appreciation. Now, since the dominant culture with which we are confronted is a traditional culture, it is above all towards tradition that the modernism discourse must be directed, so that we can effect a rereading of it and from it create a modern-day vision. Only in this way, will the modernist discourse be able to affect the large majority of the educated population, perhaps even the population as a whole, and thus fulfill its mission. As to the narcissist retirement within oneself, it can only lead to a suicidal exile and to self marginalization.

Some of our local intellectuals who claim "modernity" invoke democracy but they manage to reduce its magnitude to the mere demand of individual freedom. Simultaneously, these very persons reject rationality because it imposes "order" and puts limits on freedom. By so doing, they simply imitate certain trends of the European modernity, unaware, or pretending to be unaware, of the enormous gap that separates our condition from that of the West. It is true that in the industrialized West, rationalism has invaded and taken over all facets of individual and collective life, singly dominating human relations, the conception of the world, thought and behavior. The effects of a rational organizing of the economy, the bureaucracy, the state-apparatus, and the institutions ended up being reflected in the totality of the individual and the collective existence. The technological and computer revolutions have imposed their systematic character on all aspects of human life, thus seriously infringing upon the ethical specificity of man, perhaps even his specificity as a free being, or rather, of a being whose freedom is conditioned by his performance. Furthermore, Western rationalism has, in numerous domains, gone beyond the bounds of its own principles. It provided science and technology—which from the very rationalist point of view should have been made to serve human freedom and the right of nations (human rights)—with incredible tools for mass destruction and for the extermination of individuals, and further enabled these tools to increase and diversify their performance. Hence, the natural and justifiable human reaction, from the viewpoint of modernity, was to rise against this irrational absurdity that culminates at the of peak of modern rationalism. This revolt led some, very often for personal reasons—such as their failure of self affirmation within society—to drift away with mystical, religious or atheistic currents which made them adopt hostile positions against all forms of rationality.

Among those of us who have claimed modernity, some have espoused this irrationalist position, for the same reasons previously given, while nothing in the Arab reality can justify it. Today, the Arab world indeed suffers from the hegemony of another type of irrationality, one that is totally different from Europe's irrationalism that resulted from the European rationalism. It is a medieval irrationality, with all the consequences it implies, namely the persistence of the relationship of governor-governed where the latter, reduced to the condition of a herd, proceed with their intellectual and social lives under their shepherd's staff. Only rationalism can stand, as an effective weapon, against this backward irrationality. How do we achieve modernity without the help of reason and rationality? How do we achieve a renaissance without the help of a renewed reason? Hostility to and attacks against rationalism, in a situation like ours, can only be inspired by an irrational obscurantism. He who engages in such obscurantism inevitably condemns himself to blindness. Reason is a beacon that we must not only light in the middle of darkness but also learn to carry around well into broad daylight.

This is the conception of modernity that we ought to define in light of our present. Modernity is above all rationality and democracy. A rational and critical approach to all aspects of our existence—of which tradition emerges as one of the aspects that is most present and most rooted in us—is the only true modernist option. Our concern with tradition is therefore dictated by the necessity to elevate our approach to tradition to the level of modernity, in order to serve modernity and to give it a foundation within our "authenticity."

---

[1] This refers to the period (AH second & third centuries/ AD eighth & ninth centuries) when Muslim scholars took to the systematic codification (*tadwin*) of their transmitted knowledge, e.g., prophet's sayings (*hadith*), juridical tradition, exegeses (*tafsir*), grammar, pre-Islamic and Islamic historical traditions, etc.

PART ONE
A DIFFERENT READING
OF THE TRADITION DISCOURSE

Chapter I
The Present Shortcomings

The Fundamentalist Reading

"How do we regain the greatness of our civilization? How do we resuscitate our tradition?" These two questions closely overlap and, in their interference, make up one of the three major axes around which revolves the problematics of modern and contemporary Arab thought.

The dialogue surrounding this axis and the dialectical order that it implies are set between the past and the future. As for the present, it is not present, not only because we refuse it, but also because the past is very much present to the point that it infringes upon the future and absorbs it. Acting as the present, the past is conceived as a means to affirm and to rehabilitate one's identity.

The main reason that modern Arab consciousness affirms itself in this way is perfectly known and acknowledged. It concerns the challenge of the Western world in all its shapes. This identity affirmation, as would be the case for any individual or any society, has taken the form of a retreat to backward positions that would serve as ramparts and as defense positions. Such is the attitude held by the fundamentalist view of modern and contemporary Arab thought. This view, more than any other, sets out to resuscitate tradition, which it invested within the perspective of an heavily ideological reading, which aims at projecting a "radiant" future—fabricated by ideology—upon the past and, by the same token, "demonstrating" that "what took place in the past could be achieved in the future."

Originally, this view appeared as a religious and political move-ment—both reformist and tolerant: that of Jamal al-Din Afghani[1] and of Muhammad 'Abduh[2] This movement called for renewal (*tajdid*) against "imitative conformism" (taqlid). The rejection of imitative conformism must be herein understood with a particular meaning: i.e., "to eliminate" a whole apparatus of knowledge, of methods and of concepts inherited from the "era of decline" while being careful not to "be caught in the toils" of Western thought. As for "renewal," it was meant to create a "new" interpretation of the dogma and of the religious laws that rest directly upon the founda-tions of Islam. It was a question of actualizing *religion*, to make it contemporary and to make of it the substance of our renaissance.

It is this fundamentalist movement that brandished the banner of "authenticity" (*asala*), of one's attachment to the roots and the defense of one's identity, notions that must mean Islam itself: "the true Islam," not the Islam presently practiced by Muslims.

We are, therefore, concerned with a polemical ideological read-ing that was justifiable at the time when it was indeed a means to affirm one's identity and to reestablish confidence. It is an expres-sion of the usual defense mechanism and would perhaps continue to be legitimate, provided it remained a part of the global effort of catching up with the times. In fact, quite the opposite occurred. The means became the end: hastily reconstructed to serve as a jumping board to "glory," the past became the raison d'être for the renais-sance project. Henceforth, the future would somehow become sub-jected to a reading that used the past as a tool of interpretation, not the past that actually took place, but "the past as it should have been." But since such past existed nowhere else but in the imagination and the affective domain, the concept of the future-to-come was always unable to distance itself from the representation of the future-past. The fundamentalist lives in this representation with all his heart, not just as a romantic ideal, but also as a live reality. We would thus find him resuscitating ideological tensions from the past and implicating himself in them body and soul with the fervor of a militant. Not satisfied with adversaries from the past, he goes looking for some even into the present and the future.

The fundamentalist reading of tradition is an ahistorical one and can only provide one type of understanding of tradition: an understanding of tradition that is locked inside tradition and absorbed by a tradition that it cannot in return include: it is tradition repeating itself.

The reading of the religious fundamentalists proceeds from a religious conception of history. This conception treats history as a moment that is expanded into the present, a time that is stretched inside the affective life, a witness to the perpetual struggle and the eternal suffering endured for the sake of affirming one's identity. And since we are told that it is both faith and religious conviction that define this identity, fundamentalism posits the spiritual factor as the sole engine of history. As for the other factors, they are considered as secondary, depending upon the spiritual, or disfiguring the "true" course of history.

The Liberal Reading

"How do we live our era? How do we assume our relationship to tradition?" These are two other questions that equally overlap closely to make up, through their interference, the second axis around which revolves the problematics of modern and contemporary Arab thought. The debate around this axis and the dialectical order it implies *are set* this time between the present and the past. Not at all our own present but the Western European present which asserts itself as a "subject-ego" through which we view our era and all humankind, and therefore constitutes the "substance" of any possible future. This course of action ends up being projected on our very past and imprinting its mark on it.

The Arab liberal perception of the Arab-Islamic tradition stems from the present that it lives in, i.e., that of the West. The liberal reading is therefore European-style, which means that it adopts a European frame of reference and hence sees in tradition only what the Europeans see in it.

It is this group that espouses the orientalist discourse whose influence has been far reaching among certain Arab academics and has instilled in them an orientalist *habitus*. Its followers claim to support the scientific method, objectivity and "strict" neutrality. This reading insists that it is "disinterested" and "without any ideological intentions whatsoever."

The upholders of this *habitus* claim to be interested only in understanding and in knowledge: if indeed they do borrow the "scientific" method from the orientalists, they firmly reject their ideology. But when they say this, they forget, or pretend to forget, that along with the method they also adopt the vision. After all, are vision and method not inseparable?

The viewpoint of the orientalist method consists in confronting cultures, in reading one tradition through another. Hence the philological method which claims to bring everything back to its "origin." When it comes to reading the Arab-Islamic tradition, we would simply reconstruct it back to its Jewish, Christian, Persian, Greek, Indian, (and other) "origins."

The orientalist reading claims to want only to understand, nothing more. But what does it really seek to understand? Does it seek to understand to what extent the Arabs have "understood" the "glorious heritage" of their predecessors? Why? Is it because the contribution of the Arabs, who were the intermediaries between the Greek and the modern (European) civilizations, had no value other than having played this role? The future in the Arab past having consisted in the assimilation of a foreign past (mostly Greek Culture) into the Arab past, hence by analogy, the future in the Arab "becoming" should consist in its assimilation into the European present-past.

The modernist theses of the contemporary and modern Arab liberal thinking thus voice a dangerous identity alienation, not only that identity which is deep-rooted in a backward present, but also, and this is even worse, the identity that carries history and civilization.

The Marxist Reading

"How do we achieve our revolution? How do we restore our tradition?" These again are two questions that closely overlap and constitute, through their interference, the third and last of those main axes around which revolves the problematics of modern and contemporary Arab thought.

The debate around this axis and the dialectical order that it implies are set between the future and the past. But this is true only because both are still at the planning stage: i.e., the plan for a revolution yet to be achieved and the plan to restore a tradition capable of prodding the revolution and of becoming its foundation.

The relationship here is a dialectical one: we expect revolution to enable us to restore our tradition, and we expect tradition to contribute to our revolution. The thinking of the modern Arab left still wanders inside this vicious circle, searching for a "method" and attempting to come out.

Why?

Because it does not follow the dialectical method as a method *to be applied*, but as one that is *already applied*, whereby the Arab-Islamic cultural heritage "would have" to be the reflection of class struggle, on the one hand, and an arena of confrontation between materialism and idealism, on the other. The task of the leftist reading would hence consist in pointing out the parties involved in this double conflict and in defining their (respective) positions. Realizing its inability to accomplish its task as it "should," the leftist thinking, worried and troubled, begins to blame the situation on "the absence of a true narrative of Arab history," or to rationalize the difficulty to analyze the extreme complexity that characterizes the events of our history. Nevertheless, if some adherents to this movement insist on arbitrarily minimizing these difficulties, it is at the price of tracing historical reality over theoretical schema. Thus, unable to detect traces of a "class struggle" within this history, they invoke "historical conspiracy" and when they cannot find any scientific "materialism" in it, they then speak of an immature materialism.

This reading of the Arab-Islamic tradition by the Arab "left" leads, as a result, to a Marxist fundamentalism. It is an attempt to borrow from the founding fathers of Marxism their ready-made dialectical method, as if the goal were to prove the soundness of the ready-made method instead of applying it.

This is the reason why this reading has proven to be hardly productive.

---

[1] Jamal al-Din Afghani (died 1897). Born in Asadabad, Iran. After pursuing traditional religious studies, he went on numerous voyages throughout the whole world. He lived in Egypt where he exerted a major influence over the local intelligensia among whom he counted a disciple by the name of Muhammad 'Abduh. He was the founder of a reformist and modernist trend that was dedicated to the emancipation of the Muslim world. This movement came to be known as the *salafi* (or those who go back to the forefathers). According to him, the ultimate "takeoff" [of this movement] was to result from a combination of the positive contributions of European modernity and a purified Islamic tradition.

² Muhammad 'Abduh (1849-1905). Born in Mahallat Nasr, Egypt. After studying at the religious university of Al-Azhar, he launched his reform movement at the instigation of Afghani. He stood against the reactionary theologians and gathered many disciples around him. He became grand mufti of Egypt and reformed the religious instruction at Al-Azhar by introducing modern disciplines.

Chapter II
For a Scientific Critique of Arab Reason

In this brief overview of the most widely known readings of tradition within contemporary Arab thinking, what is important to us is not so much the defended "theses," whether adopted or "conceived" by these or those parties, but the mode of thinking that they all follow, i.e., the unconscious "mental act" that governs them. A critique that is unfamiliar with the cognitive ground upon which its subject stands remains an ideological critique of ideology and cannot therefore produce anything but ideology. What would meet the requirements of a scientific option would be a critique that would address the theoretical mode of production, i.e., the "mental act." It is a critique that would pave the way to a detached scientific reading.

If, within such perspective, we consider the three readings succinctly discussed above, we will find that from the epistemological point of view, i.e., from the point of view of the theoretical mode of functioning where all three originate, we can fault them for two major weaknesses: a weakness in method and a weakness in vision.

From the point of view of method, these readings lack the slightest necessary objectivity. From the point of view of vision, they suffer from a lack of historical perspective.

The lack of historical vision and the lack of objectivity are two closely related characteristics which influence any thought that is subjected to the tutelage of one element of the equation that it is attempting to pose: indeed any thought which, because it is incapable of becoming independent, seeks to compensate by delegating to some of the questions with which it is concerned the yardstick-role for evaluating the others. The subject then becomes absorbed into the object and the object takes the place of the subject. The latter, or what is left of it, rushes to take refuge in a remote past, seeking support from a founding ancestor, through whom and thanks to whom it can recover some self-esteem. Modern and contemporary Arab thought is part of such thinking and that is why it remains on the whole fundamentalist in its leaning, and its various schools and tendencies are in fact distinguishable only by the type of "founding ancestor" behind whom they take refuge.

Why does the fundamentalist movement permeate the whole of contemporary Arab thinking?

Thanks to the reading proposed here, we are able to observe this tendency and to trace its origins, so true is it that the rigorous and methodical examination of a subject of reading may have as its primary outcome inciting readers to revise their working tools. Let us then state what we have remarked as an indispensable introduction to the reading we are proposing.

The three readings that we have just discussed are fundamentalist, and as such they do not differ much, epistemologically speaking. All three are based upon the same reasoning mode, which the ancient Arab scholars called "analogy of the unknown after the known" (*qiyas al-gha'ib 'ala al-shahid*). And so, no matter what framework is being considered, be it religious, nationalistic, liberal or leftist, each one possesses a "known" (*shahid*) over which it will trace an "unknown" (*gha'ib*). The *unknown* in this case is the "future" as it is conceived or dreamed of by the adherents to these schools. The *known* is the first part to the double question that they all ask (e.g., for the fundamentalist movement "the greatness of our civilization", etc.).

How does this analogy work? We have no doubt that the use of analogy of the *unknown* after the *known* was once a scientific method, as long as it satisfied certain validity conditions. This method was indeed used by grammarians and jurists in their prodigious scientific work that led to the codification of the Arabic language and of the religious laws. It was borrowed by theologians who further enriched it, thanks to their debates and their terminology. It was also used by physicists who, by incorporating it in their experimental work, further added to its rigor and to its fruitfulness. In the Arab-Islamic context, it stands out as the scientific method par excellence. Scholars of all disciplines contributed to its formulation and to its codification and defined its limitations and its validity conditions. The essential conditions that guarantee the validity of analogy, as they were decreed by these scholars, may be narrowed down to the following two principles:

• analogy between two terms is only valid if they are of the same nature;

• analogy between two terms is only valid if both terms, being of the same nature, share some common element that is considered primarily a component of one and the other.

To find this "substantial component," we must resort to "detailed examination" (*sabr*) and to "analysis" (*taqsim*). Analysis consists in analyzing each one of the terms separately, i.e., enumerating all their qualities and characteristics so as to note what they possess in common. As for detailed examination, it consists in reviewing these shared qualities and characteristics so as to establish which ones are components of the substance and of the reality of both terms. Analysis represents an analytical procedure while detailed examination is a method of review and verification that somewhat corresponds to Francis Bacon's "crucial experience."

That methodological approach was thus a rigorous and, as much as possible, a cautious one. But, because of the preponderance that it acquired and of the great predilection with which it was utilized, it ended up being popularized to the point where people became progressively less careful about its validity conditions. And so, the casual use of an expression like "deduce the rest..." ultimately resulted in a dispensation from any depth in research. That technique in analogy remained so deeply anchored in the exercise of Arab reason that it became the sole "mental act" on which the production of knowledge has rested.

For example, within jurisprudence (*fiqh*), scholars tended to abuse analogy to the point where it became impossible for them to strictly abide by its validity conditions: case-applications (cases-in-point) of the sources/foundations[1] became adopted as sources from which new case-applications (cases-in-point) were deduced and in turn transformed into sources. This way, analogical reasoning became a mechanical operation such that it was difficult, if not impossible, to submit it to the exigencies of "detailed examination" and to "analysis." In the area of dialectical theology (*kalam*),[2] as far as the theologians were concerned, what they called "analogical reasoning" (*istidlal bi al-shahid 'ala al-gha'ib*) remained always unfounded. Jurists were able to base their practice of analogy on a common rule—stating that the finality of any legal opinion (*hukm*) had to be "the consideration of the common good and the removal of prejudice"—a practice that allowed them to share a common base for their debates and their controversies. Theologians, on the other hand, who were unable to agree on a comparable rule, singly resorted to their own ways to justify their respective analogies. Each one then abusively assigned to "*in praesentia* referents" (known) certain qualities for the sole purpose of justifying their analogical connection with "*in absentia* referents" (unknown), thus altering, according to the circumstances, the "contents" and the manner of "how to contain." The result of this was to prolong the polemics ad infinitum without any benefit whatsoever. As for grammarians, even if, to justify their procedures, they were able to agree on a common rule affirming that the Arabic language is essentially characterized by a "fluidity of expression," they too accumulated analogies. All things considered, their work became an end in itself, therefore deviating from its primary function, i.e., to codify the language, and in the process complicating to excess this language which was originally "simple" and "spontaneous."

Indeed, during the final stages of its development, the practice of analogy by grammarians, jurists and theologians ended up "snowballing" and becoming deeply rooted in the structure of the Arab reason, both as a mode of thinking and as a principle of "activity." thus giving way to the mechanical and unconscious practice of analogy. And if on top of this we consider that the cultural activity at the time of the "decline" was almost exclusively limited to rolling this "snowball"—since the only scholarly practices left were those of grammar, law and the "science of oneness" (theology)—we would understand how analogy became a mental operation that was practiced unconsciously by the Arabs and therefore without any attention whatsoever to its validity conditions. Subsequently, every unknown object became some analogy's *in absentia* term to which one had to relate an *in praesentia* term (known) at any price. And since the supreme "unknown" is most assuredly the future, and the past alone is known (or at least we believe that it is), the mental activity that sought to resolve the questions of "present" and "past" was limited, almost exclusively, to seeking those elements from the past that could be analogically related to the present. Thus, the practice of "analogy from the known to the unknown"—this scientific method that had been the logical-methodological basis for the Arab-Islamic sciences—turned into a practice that related the new to the old by analogy. Knowing the new would therefore mean "discovering" an old to which we could relate the new.

The influence on the thinking by this mental device, which had become the *modus operandi* within the productive activity of the Arab reason, subsequently produced major consequences:

• the suspension of the notions of tenses and of evolution. Every present became systematically related to the past, as if past, present

and future were in fact a smooth stretch or an immobile time; hence the absence of historical perspective from the Arab thinking;
• the absence of disjunction between the subject and the object. By abandoning "detailed examination" and "analysis," they turned the analogical process into a mental device incapable of focusing on the analysis of analogical terminology or on the examination of its components in order to draw similarities. Analogy was therefore used mechanically, without research or analysis, without examination or critique. The *in praesentia* referent settled in as a witness that is permanently present inside reason and emotions; hence the absence of objectivity from the Arab thinking.

The entirety of modern and contemporary Arab thought is characterized by a lack of historical perspective and objectivity. And that is why it was never able to offer from tradition anything but a fundamentalist reading that treats the past as transcendental and sacral while seeking to extract from it ready-made solutions to the problems of the present and the future. If such a remark perfectly applies to the Islamists, it is no less applicable to the other schools of thought all of which claim their own founding fathers with whom they can find "salvation." All the schools of Arab thought seem to borrow their prospect for renewal from a past-related (or past-based) model: the Arab-Islamic past, the European "past-present," the Russian experience, the Chinese one...and one could extend the list. When facing a new problem, this kind of thought resorts to the mechanical mental exercise of seeking ready-made solutions, relying on a rather poor "foundation."

But this mental exercise is part of a whole, even if it is an essential part of it. This whole is the structure of the Arab reason. It is therefore this reason that we ought to submit to careful analysis and to rigorous critique, before proposing its renewal and its modernization. The Arab reason can only be renewed through a serious questioning of the old and through a global and in-depth critique, to which I hope to have made a modest contribution with my work: *Naqd al-'aql al-'Arabi*.[3]

Methodological Questions of a Disjunctive-"Rejunctive" Reading

(a) About the necessity of a break-away from an understanding of tradition that is locked inside tradition

The foregoing remarks were meant to draw the attention to the fact that the first methodological question that contemporary Arab thought would have to deal with, in its attempts to conceive an "adequate" method of assuming its relationship to tradition, would be—rather than knowing how to choose between such or such readymade method—examining the mental operation that directs the application of a method, whatever it may be. Before we set out to practice our reason in any fashion, we must submit to a critique.

Today's Arab reason is a structure within which many components come to play, namely the type of "theoretical practice" (grammatical, juridical, theological) prevalent during the "era of decline," and the constituent order of which was [the use of] analogy of the unknown after the known as it was practiced without any attention to its conditions of scientific validity. This irresponsible practice of analogy has become the invariable element (the constant) that regulates the movements within the structure of Arab reason. This element stops time, suspends evolution and creates a permanent presence of the past inside the game of thought and inside the affective domain, thus feeding the present with ready-made solutions. The "renewal of Arab thought" or the "modernization of Arab reason" are in my opinion condemned to remain a dead letter as long as we do not volunteer, first of all, to break the structure of this reason that we inherited from the "era of decline." The first object to de-construct—by means of a severe and rigorous criticism—will have to be the structural constant of this reason, the mechanical practice of analogy as we described it. To renew Arab reason is, from within our perspective, to effect a decisive epistemological break from the structure of the Arab reason of the "era of decline" and its extension in modern and contemporary Arab thinking.

But what do we mean by "epistemological break"? Let me make it clear right away that the epistemological break by no means takes place at the level of knowledge itself. It has therefore nothing to do with those pernicious theses that call for locking up tradition inside museums or for confining it in a "remote" historical past where its place would be limited. This automatic rejection of tradition is a nonscientific and an ahistorical attitude. It is even paradoxically a residue of the thinking on tradition during the "era of decline." The epistemological break takes place at the level of the mental act, i.e., the unconscious activity that is practiced inside a given cognitive field, according to a given order and by means of given cognitive tools: the concepts. Knowledge remains there. It is the way we treat knowledge that changes; the mental tools utilized; the problematics dictated by this activity and the cognitive field where it becomes organized. When change proves to be too profound and too radical so that we can say that a point of no return has been reached, a point from which we can no longer return to the earlier way of treating knowledge, we will then speak of an epistemological break.

I am by no means calling for a break from tradition—in the usual sense. Rather, we are calling for renouncing traditional understanding of tradition. In other words, we must eliminate in our way of understanding tradition the residues of tradition that have settled within us, and especially that grammatical-juridical-theological analogy—practiced irresponsibly in a nonscientific way. That practice consists in establishing mechanical relationships between the parts and contributes thereby to disrupting the cohesion of the whole and to subtracting the different parts of the whole from their historical-cognitive-ideological setting, in order to move the parts of this whole into another whole: the field to which belongs the practitioner of analogy, causing a fusion of subject and object. That fusion will lead either to distorting the object, or to unconsciously implicating the subject into the object, and very often to both at the same time. *A fortiori* when it comes to tradition, the consequence of this will be the complete fusion of the subject into the object-tradition.

But it is another thing for the subject to blend in with tradition, another one to go along with tradition; another one to become absorbed by tradition and yet another one to assimilate tradition. The break that we wishfully call for is not one from tradition but from a certain kind of relationship to tradition. This break must transform us from those beings "taken by tradition" to those beings who have embraced their tradition, i.e., personalities with a tradition that happens to make up one of their own components, which will enable the person to find his/her membership inside a larger personality, that of the community which has inherited this tradition.

The question of method does not face us in terms of a choice between a historicist, a functionalist, a structuralist or other method... In fact, each could be perfectly valid in one area without necessarily being so in another. But all remain useless so long as we have not established the necessary disjunction between the object and the subject, so long as the object does not enjoy its own (relative) independence, so that the subject and the object do not interfere in each other's geneses in a direct way. *A fortiori* when the object that we are treating is as eminently a part of the subject—and the subject is as eminently a part of the object—as tradition, the methodological challenge to be noted as a priority is therefore to find the means to disjoin the subject from the object and to disjoin the object from the subject, in order to allow for the rebuilding of their relationship on a new basis.

The question of method is therefore, first and foremost, a question of objectivity.

(b) About disjoining the "read-object" from the "subject-reader": the problem of objectivity

How do we create an objective understanding of tradition? This is in our opinion the essential methodological question that faces contemporary Arab thought in its attempts to devise an adequate scientific method to assume its relationship to tradition. Here, it is not only a question of "objectivity" in the normal sense of the term (the absence of implication of the subject, with its desires and its impulses, into the object). The kind of relationship that exists today between the Arab self and its tradition requires that we understand the problem of objectivity from these two frameworks:

• the framework of the relationship of subject versus object, in which case objectivity shall consist in disjoining the object from the subject;
• the framework of the relationship of object versus subject, in which case objectivity shall consist in disjoining the subject from the object.

The first of these disjunctions is conditioned by the second one.

In the reading of tradition that I am proposing, why do I insist so much on disjunction between subject and object? Because the contemporary Arab "reader" is restricted by his tradition and overwhelmed by his present, which means first of all that tradition absorbs him, thus depriving him of independence and of freedom. From the day of his birth, we have not ceased to instill tradition in him, in the form of a certain vocabulary and certain concepts, of a language and a thought; in the form of fables, legends and imaginary representations, of a certain kind of relationship to things and a certain way of thinking; of certain types of knowledge and certain truths. He receives all this without the slightest critical reaction or critical mind. It is through these instilled principles that he will conceive of things, and on them will base his opinions and observations. The practice of thought under these circumstances becomes more a game of reminiscence. When the Arab reader pores over the texts of tradition, his reading of these texts will therefore be evocative, rather than exploratory and reasoned.

It is true that a nation cannot think the world except through its tradition. But it is one thing to think through a tradition that has known a continuous evolution into the present, a tradition of which the present is an integral part, a tradition that has been continuously renewed, revised and critiqued. And it is another thing to think through a tradition whose evolution was interrupted centuries ago, a tradition that is removed from the present by the deep gap that progress and science have dug between it and the present.

Let us consider, for example, the relationship of the Arab reader to the Arabic language, which happens to be at the same time the material of the old text and the tool used by the reader to read. This language, remaining the same for over fourteen centuries, has shaped culture and thought without being in return shaped by them. And thus it has continued to be the element most rooted in tradition and in authenticity. Hence its sacral character.

The Arabic language absorbs the reader because it exerts on him a sacral influence and because it is part of his taboos. When, as an adult, he reads an Arabic text, he will read the language rather than the text. What is more shocking for an Arab reader than a discourse where the meaning does not blend in with the style, and where the style does not blend in with the language? Only the usual "abundant" and "eloquent" discourse can guarantee his peace of mind and the satisfaction of an easy enunciation. He likes this fluid discourse where the meaning blends in with the style; this discourse which is easily assimilable because its significance obtains from its musicality.

Furthermore, the Arab reader is overwhelmed by his present so he goes searching, inside his tradition, for some guarantors upon whom he could project his hopes and his aspirations. As he mistakes dream for reality, he hopes to find in tradition "science," "rationality," "progress," etc., in a word everything that neither dream nor reality can offer him in his present. Because of this reason, we see him rushing the meaning of the words in the direction of expectations. By picking certain things along the way and turning his back on the others, he therefore breaks the unity of the text, perverts its meaning and moves it out of its cognitive and historical contexts.

The contemporary Arab reader lives under the stress of having to be abreast of his times. But the more his era escapes him, the more he seeks to reinforce the affirmation of his identity and to seek magical solutions to his numerous problems. Although he may be absorbed by tradition, he makes every effort to adjust its absorption in such a way that its "reading" will flash him back the image of everything he was unable to fulfill. He makes the text tell about his own concerns before reading what the text says.

To disjoin the subject from his tradition is therefore a necessary operation. This operation represents the first step towards an objective attitude. The methodological achievements in the field of modern linguistics can provide us with an objective method to distance ourselves from the texts, a method that we could sum up through he following golden rule: "One must avoid interpreting the meaning of the text before grasping its material (material as a network of relationships between the units of meaning, and not as a set of units of isolated meanings)." We must free ourselves of any understanding built upon biases derived from tradition or upon our present-day desiderata. We must put all of this between parentheses so as to devote ourselves to the sole task of noting the significance of the text within the text itself., i.e., within the network of the relationships that are created among its elements. Treating the text as a network of relationships and devoting ourselves to determining the interplay of these relationships will enable us to stop the "fluttering of those countless threads" that reduce the words of the Arabic language, in the eyes of the reader, to some melodies, some pure sensitive forms or some receptacles for all sensations and all passions. In other words, in order to free ourselves of the text, we must submit it to a meticulous dissection that will turn the text into an object for the subject-reader, a material with a reading.

Disjoining the subject from the object is perhaps necessary, but this operation is only a first step that will enable the subject to regain its dynamism in order to rebuild the object in a new perspective. The second step that we must take towards objectivity is the one that consists in disjoining the object from the subject so that the object can in turn regain its independence and its "personality," its identity and its historicity.

This process is made up of three phases:

• *The Structuralist Approach.* It consists in treating what was produced by the author of the text as a whole that is governed by certain constants and enriched by those transformations supported by the author's thinking around the same axis. The author's thinking needs to be basically focused around a prominent problematics that is willing to accept all those transformations within which the author's thinking moves, so that every one of his ideas finds its natural place— i.e., justified or justifiable—within the whole. This may be a difficult operation, but if care is taken to link the author's ideas together, if attention is paid to the expressive devices that are put forth and if note is made of the discourse recipients, we can manage to tackle it with more ease.

• *The Historical Approach.* It essentially consists in linking the author's thinking, whose internal organization would have already been restored, to its historical context in its cultural, ideological, political and social dimensions. This "inclusion in history" is indispensable, not only to acquire a historical understanding of the thinking under study, but also to test the validity of the structuralist model offered in the previous approach. By "validity" we do not mean, here, the logical veracity (the non-contradiction) of the model—in fact this has already been established, partially at least, by the structuralist approach—but rather its historical possibility, i.e., that which guarantees to us what a given text can or cannot contain. This way, we will be able to conceive what the text could have said but did not reveal.

• *The Ideological Approach.* The historical analysis could remain an incomplete and purely pro forma work without the recourse to the ideological approach of the text, i.e., to the updating of the ideological (sociopolitical) function that a (given) thought fulfills, seeks to fulfill or that someone wanted to make it fulfill, within the cognitive field of which it is a part. We must now lift the parentheses within which the structuralist analysis had for a while confined—by synchronizing it—the historical period of which the text is a part, in order to give its life back to the era. To note the ideological content of a thought is the only way indeed to make it contemporary to itself, and to link it to the world to which it belongs.

Disjoining the subject from the object and the object from the subject are two interdependent operations; we have only dissociated them for the sake of exposition. Together, they represent the first methodological concern, that of objectivity.

But is it enough to be objective in order to read tradition? The read-object is indeed our tradition. It is not simply and solely to get rid of it that we have just extirpated this part from ourselves, nor is it to enjoy—as an ethnologist would—the spectacle of its cultural or architectural achievements, nor is it to behold its abstract conceptual edifices—as a philosopher would—but rather to re-join it to us in a new form and under a new relationship, so that we may make it contemporary to us.

But how do we bring about such "rejunction"?

(c) About rejoining the read-object to the subject-reader: the problem of continuity

Tradition is not only a product of history, shaped only by history and society. It is also the sum of personal contributions that we owe to certain persons who have marked history because they knew, at least in part, how to free themselves of the shackles of history and society. But more often than not, these contributions do not reveal themselves in a direct manner. The moral or material pressures exerted by society present just as many shackles to the contributions of certain people who hold new ideas and "seditious" aspirations. They prevent these people from expressing themselves openly and directly. Their ideas press on and rush behind the predominant schema of thought and modes of writing, settling in a deep zone, beyond speech (beyond logic). Therefore, we can only reach these ideas when we cross the limits of speech and of logic.

This can only be achieved through intuition, the only thing capable of making the read-self embrace the reading-self, of making the former participate in the problematics and concerns of the latter and of making it interested in its aspirations. The reading-self will seek to find itself inside the read-self, yet fully conserving the identity of the latter. This way, the reading-self, on its own, will be able to entirely maintain its conscience and its personality. The intuition we are talking about here is by no means that of the mystics, nor is it Bergsonian or personalist, nor a phenomenological one, but a particular kind of intuition, a mathematical intuition of sorts. It is about the immediate and exploratory representation that unlocks evidence, provides an anticipated understanding in the course of a dialogue between the reading-self and the read-self created on the basis of objective data that emanate from the first one of our methodological concerns.

It is this kind of intuition which enables the reading-self to unearth what the read-self had silenced. To this end, intuition must decipher signs within the text—*undoubtedly* folded inside the game of thought—that are hidden by the strategy of discourse. We must not suspend logic. On the contrary, we must push the logic of the text to the end, in order to draw the necessary conclusions resulting from the premises and the combinations that it supports.

At this level, conclusions are what enables reading to imagine the premises; the future is what enables reading to imagine the past; what *was supposed to be* that enables reading to imagine what *was*. Hence, the positiveness of what *was* blends in with the ideological of what *was supposed to be*, and the future-past to which the read-self aspired becomes the future-to-come that the reading-self pursues. Hence, the read-object which is contemporary to itself becomes contemporary to the subject-reader.

Why must we resort to this kind of intuition in the reading of our philosophical tradition, and why worry about having access to the un-said? It is within tradition itself and among our thinkers that we can find an answer to our question: Ghazali[4] mentions a book that he had supposedly written under the title: *What We Never Divulge to Those Who Are Not Apt for It*. This particular work has not reached us and it is even highly probable that he never wrote it. Avicenna,[5] himself, had also spoken of a book entitled *Oriental* (Eastern) *Philosophy*, in which he claimed to have presented his true doctrine. But this book never reached us, either; and it seems that the philosopher may have kept it in his possession like a secret that "we never divulge to those who are not apt for it." As for Averroes,[6] he evokes a certain "demonstrative wisdom" that—in his words—we must attempt "only to acquire in the appropriate places." Access to this wisdom must be limited only to those who are apt for it and it cannot be spread among the masses. This wisdom was also one of those which "we must never divulge to those who are not apt for it." Well before these, al-Farabi[7] had already spoken of a "truth" and of "allegories of truth" and advised that we decipher the truth from beyond its allegories. Other thinkers, such as Jabir Ibn Hayyan[8] and the physician Rhazès[9] mentioned similar things. All our philosophers, therefore, kept some ideas to themselves, which they would not divulge to those who were not apt for them, if not by allusions, by symbols, or "from behind a veil."

"What we do not divulge to those who are not apt for it?" therefore occupies in their texts the space of a "that" which we must try to unveil. And we can only do this by deliberately engaging in their problematics and in their intellectual pursuits. But are we free to reveal publicly today what our ancestors made sure not to divulge to those who were not apt for it, perhaps even what they could not reveal to themselves? To realize all that this question implies enables us to become their contemporaries and to make them contemporary to us on the level of a spirit aware of its historicity. It is through such "inter-contemporaneity" that continuity is achieved: continuity in the evolution of consciousness through a quest for truth.

Elements of a Vision, Principles of a Reading

Whether we want it or not, every method necessarily proceeds from a vision. In order to validly implement a method, it is imperative to be aware of the perspectives of the vision from which it proceeds. This is because vision represents the framework of the method and defines its perspectives, in the same way that the method contributes to enhancing and readjusting vision.

After having described our methodological approach, let us unveil at this time the different components of our vision. They are the ones that shape the constancies upon which is based the reading that we propose and through which our reading finds direction. We will summarize them here under three aspects.

(a) Unity of thought: unity of the problematics

I proceed from the principle that theoretical thinking in a given society at a given time constitutes a particular unity endowed with its own armature inside of which the different movements and tendencies blend in, so to speak. From this point of view, it is the whole which is significant, and not the components. The latter are mere aspects of a homogeneous whole.

It is with this in mind that we can speak of, say, Greek thought despite the multiplicity of tendencies that shape it, or of contemporary Arab thought, despite the diversity of its schools. And it is also with this in mind that we can speak of medieval Arab-Islamic thought in spite of the apparent plurality and the apparent differences that characterize it. We thus consider these great moments of Arab thought as irreducible units, likely to be studied as such, each as a whole. But what constitutes the unity of this whole?

The unity of a system of thought, from our perspective, is not defined according to its authors' belonging to the same community (national, religious, linguistic, etc.) , or according to the identity of the studied topics, or the membership in such a thought system within a common spatial-temporal perimeter. Unity of thought simply means *unity of the problematics*. Whether or not the authors of such thought dealt with identical topics, whether or not they reached the same conclusions, whether or not they lived in the same period, under the same sky or in different geographical regions, is not at all significant, in my opinion, since this is not a decisive factor in creating unity of thought. What determines and creates unity of thought, at a given historical period, is the unity of problematics within this thought.

But let me clarify this statement by making the meaning of the word "problematics," in this context, more explicit. A problematics is a network of relationships, inside a given thought system, woven around a set of problems that interact in such a way that it is impossible to resolve them in isolation and that—on the theoretical level— can only be resolved globally. In other words, a problematics is a theory whose conditions for its creation are not yet met; it is a theory in the making, a propensity towards the stabilization of thought.

Let us illustrate this definition with a familiar example: the example of what is called "modern Arab thought", i.e., that of the "Arab Renaissance" *(nahda)*. This thought system indeed constitutes a unity because it deals with one and the same problematics, the problematics of Renaissance *(nahda)*. We are speaking of a problematics of Renaissance rather than a problem of Renaissance. In fact, what preoccupied Arab thinkers of the "Renaissance period" was not a single problem, but rather a web of overlapping problems that are impossible to resolve in isolation, or even to analyze each singly without linking it to the others (e.g., European invasion, Turkish despotism, poverty, illiteracy, education, language, the status of women, the lack of national unity, etc.)

When dealing with these problems, Arab thought during the Renaissance period perceived them globally. When raising one of them, it necessarily had to raise all the others, or at least deal with some of their aspects. For within a given problematics, it is less the problem in itself which is of importance than is the function served by this problem as an element of the problematics. Let us consider, for example, the way Qasim Amin[10] dealt with the problem of the status of women. What concerned him more was not the "woman" as an isolated entity but the promotion of the woman as a Renaissance factor, where emancipation represented a stake within the problematics of the Renaissance; when he had to analyze the status of Arab women, he was forced to deal with the problems of education, democracy, tradition and customs, language, in short, to deal with the global problematics of the Renaissance.

The unity or the universality of a thought system can be noted both in the global production of the authors of this thought and in the work of a single one. In other words, the unity of thought, in so far as it is determined by the unity of the problematics, fashions itself in the same way on the level of the era—which represents the specific historical field where the work of all the period's thinkers had been produced—as it does on the level of the *oeuvre* of any one of these. That is why it is necessary, when reading the *oeuvre* of an author, to think of it as a part of the intellectual output of the historical period-field of which it is a part.

We must further add that the problematics of a given thought system generally goes beyond the borders of its actual output and extends to the totality of the possible ways of thinking within the field of this thought. A plurality of views does not necessarily mean a plurality of problematics. Different thinkers who are members of the same problematics might ask different questions, but their answers to these questions will likely be identical, similar or complementary. Conversely, the questions might be identical, but the answers offered will be divergent. Sometimes, there will be questions that no one will answer, and someone will answer questions that have not been asked. By no means do all these phenomena cut into the unity of the problematics; on the contrary, they reveal its fecundity, its coherence and its power of integration of a great number of ways of thinking. In other words, the field of a problematics is not limited only to the problems that it expresses but includes all its unexpressed potentialities. And this why a problematics does not necessarily remain confined inside a spatial-temporal perimeter; it remains open to taking in any subsequent output that has not gone obsolete. (We can say, for example, that the problematics of conciliation of transmission [*naql*] and reason [*'aql*], inside which the medieval Arab thinking fit, has remained open to this day, or rather that it was reopened at the time of the Arab Renaissance, since up to now, a number of persons still persist in thinking of it under the same conditions as medieval people did.)

(b) Historicity of thought: cognitive field and ideological content

The previous remarks lead us to the tackling of the second constancy of vision which informs our reading of the philosophical output within Islamic thinking: historicity of thought, i.e., its relationship to the political, sociological, economical and cultural realities of which it is a product, or at least in the midst of which it evolved.

When we make the statement that a problematics is not confined inside a spatial-temporal perimeter, that it remains open to taking in any subsequent output that has not become obsolete, we are made to question ourselves about the relationship between thought and reality and, therefore, between thought and history. Indeed, there exists between these two phenomena a complex relation, not that it is unanalyzable but because it remains irreducible to preconceived schema and that it requires that we adjust its analysis so as to fully understand the relation. The historical field of a thought system does not necessarily correspond to a period-based history, i.e., according to dynastic successions, economic mutations, wars or other non-necessarily determinant factors to the evolution of this thought. The relative—but nevertheless very often real—independence of this thought vis-à-vis these factors compels us to resort to those components that are inherent to the thought itself in order to grasp its historical field. What we mean here by "historical field" of a thought system corresponds in fact to the "duration of the life of a problematics," or to its "era": it is a period during which the same problematics persists in the history of a given thought.

The historical field of a thought is defined according to two criteria:

• *the cognitive field* which circumscribes the movement of a thought and is made up of a homogeneous "cognitive material," hence of a homogeneous conceptual apparatus (notions, concepts, method, vision, etc.);

• *the ideological content* which this thought carries, i.e., the ideological function (socio-political) to which the author or authors of this thought subordinate the cognitive material.

To be able to define the kind of relation that exists between these two criteria and, therefore, the links that one must create between thought and reality, one must conceive that the theoretical problematics—which makes up the unity of thought—is fundamentally of a cognitive nature, insofar as it is the result of the coexistence of contradictions inside a given cognitive field. Thus it will persist as long as the positive epistemological conditions that determine this cognitive field remain in place. Whereas the ideological contents, in view of which this cognitive material is used, are not the result of this type of contradictions, but of another type of contradictions and of (ideological) conflicts that do not take root/originate in the degree of evolution of a cognitive apparatus, but in the stage of evolution of a society. And since the evolution of knowledge does not necessarily follow the same pace as that of society, the cognitive and ideological contents that are articulated by the same thought are not necessarily concomitant. In most cases the pace of one is either slower or faster than that of the other. In other words, to be a part of the same problematics and a part of the same cognitive field does not *de facto* imply a commitment to the same ideology, or that the material offered by this cognitive field is used for the same ideological goals. Often, it is even the opposite, the same cognitive system, perhaps even the same idea, can articulate opposite ideological contents.

Consequently, if it is relatively easy to associate one philosopher's thinking with the cognitive field of which he is a member—with the help of data provided by the history of science and knowledge in general—we cannot, on the other hand, when pointing out the ideological content promoted by the thinking, consult nothing else but this thought alone. Indeed, the social or political ambitions, reflected by a given ideology, do not on the whole coincide historically: neither with the cognitive material handled by this ideology, nor with the evolutionary moment of the society in which it manifests itself. Furthermore, if we think that philosophy is by nature one of the most abstract ways of thinking possible, that it has a tendency to "purify," to the maximum the material provided by the cognitive field, we will readily understand to what degree the relationship of philosophical thinking versus socio-historical reality can prove to be a complex one. It is very often an indirect relationship, borrowing the way of other forms of consciousness—religious or political—and reflecting aspirations that are conceived outside the spatial-temporal perimeter, either ahead of or behind their time. It is according to these aspirations that the thinker will use the cognitive material at his disposal to finally represent them in the shape of an output that aims at being purely scientific.

(c) Islamic philosophy: readings of Greek philosophy

Our insistence on the necessity to distinguish between cognitive and ideological contents that are articulated by the same thought does not stem only from a methodological necessity. It is the reality of philosophical thinking in Islam that dictate it to us. All the Muslim philosophers' creative activity centered around one problematics, which is usually referred to as the problematics of "reconciling reason and transmission." First the Mu'tazilites[11] raised this question by launching their credo: "Reason takes precedence over the transmitted data." Then came the school of the Eastern philosophers, which reached its peak with the person of Avicenna,[12] whose spokesmen never ceased to work at incorporating the structure of "scientific" (Greek) thinking to that of (Islamic) religious thinking, driven by the conviction that the first one represented the rational and "scientific" conception of man and the universe, and the second one represented "absolute" truth, as well as cultural identity.

The possibilities of innovation in the hands of the Muslim philosophers were therefore very limited. Philosophers did not read their predecessors with the perspective of completing the work of the latter, or to go beyond them. Being all of them readers of yet other philosophers, the Greek ones (particularly Plato and Aristotle), they in fact give an outside observer—who would restrict his study of their output only from the standpoint of the cognitive material it disseminates—the impression of simply repeating one another. In other words, what we call "Islamic philosophy" did not enjoy a continual and renewed reading of its own history like Greek philosophy or like the European philosophy from Descartes until now. Philosophy in Islam has always been based on individual readings having a foreign philosophy (Greek philosophy) for object. These readings have vested the same cognitive material with diverse ideological aims.

We ought to distinguish between the ideological content and the cognitive content in Islamic philosophy to be able to detect the variety, the dynamic and the expanse of this thought, and to replace it within the context of its socio-historical commitments. Those who—following the example of the majority of observers—limit themselves to looking at it from the standpoint of the cognitive content (scientific and metaphysical) will only find ever-"rehashed" opinions and discourses that may differ only in the way their authors present them, focus on such or such theme, or in the extent of their brevity. Whether they admit it or not, they will ultimately acknowledge the sterility of such thinking. But if we were to consider philosophical thinking in Islam from the standpoint of the ideology that it articulates, we would realize that we are dealing with an evolving thought, governed by its own principles and its own problematics and full of fertile contradictions.

The biggest mistake made by historians of Islamic thought, be they from the old days or from the modern era, be they orientalists or Arabs, was to always look at it strictly through its cognitive content. That is why they never found in it enough material to write a living and dynamic history. In his *kitab al-Milal wa al-Nihal*, Shahrastani[13] saw in philosophy a mere succession of repetitive discourses; consequently, he presented the doctrines of philosophers through one single book, Avicenna's *kitab al-Najat*. Most of the orientalists, for their part, saw in it nothing but "Greek philosophy written in Arabic characters." Even those among them who wished to avoid the judgment formulated by E. Renan[14]—though void of historical logic—in the end showed the history of Islamic philosophy as a mere repetition of the history of Greek philosophy, restaging the division among the schools of the latter and retracing the various phases of its evolution. It was thus decreed that there had been Islam's very own "naturalists," "Pythagoreans," and adepts of Plato and Aristotle who were reread by neo-platonists of the likes of T. J. De Boer[15] who remained nonetheless one of the best orientalists to have written on the subject. As for some contemporary Arab researchers, they followed Shahrastani's path by rereading Muslim philosophers through only one of their representatives (either Avicenna or Farabi), if not by simply imitating DeBoer in the way he assimilated Islamic philosophy to Greek philosophy, and often for that matter without as much intelligence as their master or his translator-commentator Abu Rida. Though there may have been a few recent attempts to go beyond the method of the old scholars or beyond that of the modern orientalists and their students, these have remained confined inside the preconceived schemas and have used the dialectical method as an "already-applied-method" rather than as a method to-be-applied. These attempts led to a writing of history of Islamic thought that blindly reproduced the general evolution of human thought, blending the particular with the general; a history where the specific no longer had any other vocation but to serve as a justification for the validity of the method.

All the mistakes made about the history of Islamic philosophy are nothing but the result of the confusion between the cognitive and the ideological contents of this philosophy. And since it is the cognitive content which is expressed with most immediacy in the texts, and since it is the one directly borrowed from the Greek philosophy and sciences, those responsible for this confusion could not help but present philosophical thinking in Islam as an inert body and its contributions as faded copies of the Greek "originals" or of the originals of universal thought. After all, those who wanted to read a semblance of dynamics in these copies could not do it without closely copying Islamic thought after the preconceived schema that made up their credo and after whose model they redrew reality. Generally speaking, the cognitive and the ideological contents in Greek philosophy experienced a parallel evolution; for the former thanks to scientific progress, for the latter thanks to the evolution of society. From the time of Thales to the time of Aristotle, so many stages went by in which scientific consciousness and ideological consciousness had evolved hand in hand. This parallelism is even more striking in modern European thought. By contrast, throughout the Greek antiquities and throughout the medieval era, in Christendom as in Islam, the cognitive material vested in philosophical thought remained unchanged. The only thing that changed was the ideological use that was made of it.

That does not mean that science did not evolve at all during the era of the Arab-Islamic enlightenment. The formidable advances made at that time (e.g., in the field of mathematics thanks to Khawarizmi,[16] to al-Karkhi,[17] and to Samaw'al al-Maghribi,[18]; in the field of astronomy thanks to Battani[19]; in the field of medicine thanks to Rhazes,[20] Avicenna, and others) indeed enabled science throughout the Arab-Islamic history to go through some essential evolutionary stages. These advances—because they could not—did not impact the predominant conceptions of that period's philosophers.

There are two reasons that explain why philosophers did not have to undergo the influence of these scientific advances:

(1) the fact that the advances in scientific research made at that time never truly went beyond the inherited cognitive field within which these advances were no more than the extension of a prior scientific knowledge ;

(2) the fact that Muslim philosophers concerned themselves, priority-wise, less with producing conceptions based on new substance, than with reconciling the religious conception of the world to reason, and to justifying rational conception from a religious standpoint. This is why Islamic philosophy was continually an ideological discourse and why those who remain deaf to such a discourse, looking at Islamic philosophy with the same eye as they would Greek philosophy or European philosophy, are doomed to remember from it only an "immobile" void of progress and of dynamics.

Islamic philosophy was never the subject of a sustained and renewed reading of its own history, its own epistemological and metaphysical gains. It was always based upon various readings of a foreign philosophy, i.e. the Greek philosophy. Therefore, the contributions of Islamic philosophy to renewal must not be sought in the cognitive gains it has vested and spread, but in the ideological function that each philosopher assigns to this knowledge. It is there that we can find a meaning and a history to Islamic philosophy.

---

[1] At the time when the various juridical schools were created, jurists would relate by analogy the new cases that arose from concrete daily life to principles articulated by the Qur'an and by the Prophet's sayings. The first ones are called *far'* (cases in point, case applications) and the second ones are called *asl* (foundation/source). After these juridical schools became established, each group of adherents started to relate "new cases" from their own era to "new cases" from the era of the leaders of their respective schools. Subsequently, their later successors began to treat as foundations/sources those "new cases" previously considered as " cases in point" and deduce new analogies after them.

[2] The rationale behind *kalam* was the defensive vindication of the Muslim religion. The origin of the practice of *kalam* is tied to various political-religious debates over the legitimacy of the regime, free will and predestination during the second century (AH), eighth century (AD). *Kalam* began to develop in Baghdad under the Abbassids when classical Greek philosophy and science were introduced. As schools of *kalam* (first the Mu'tazilits, then the Ash'arits) began to take

shape, one noted the active participation of the ruling caliphs who, at times, adopted very harsh positions. On the theoretical level, the science of *kalam* gave rise to the development of metaphysical notions and a discourse over the relationship between God, man and the universe: oneness of God, divine transcendence, the question of divine justice, the question of the Qur'an being "created" or "noncreated," the *ex nihilo* creation of the world, etc.

[3] The translation of this important work is forthcoming.

[4] Abu Hamid Muhammad al-Ghazali (450-505/1059-1111) was known in the medieval Western World under the name of Algazel. He is one of the most representative thinkers of Islam, as suggested by his honorific nickname of *Hujjat al-Islam* (the proof, the guarantor of Islam). He was born near Tus in Khurasan (eastern Iran), twenty-three years after the death of Avicenna. His training as a youth was marked by his contacts with the great schools of thought of the time: philosophy, esoterism, theology. He was a disciple of Juwayni, the most prominent Ash'arite theologian of his time who was nicknamed *Imam al-Haramayn*. He was called to the court of Nizam al-Mulk, vizier to the Seljukid Sultans whose dynasty (of Turkish origin) had taken over the Abbassid Caliphate under the cover of protecting it from the Fatimid expansion. Ghazali was charged with instructing Ash'arite Kalam in a teaching institution founded by Nizam al-Mulk in Baghdad, the *Madrasa Nizamiyya*. In his intellectual "autobiography," entitled *Al-Munqidh min al-Dalal* (Deliverance from Deviation), Ghazali tells of the inner crisis caused by his "doubts" towards all the knowledge that he had acquired and which he was charged with teaching. "Deliverance is said to have come to him from Sufism, from the spiritual realization which he later tried to accommodate to the dogma of Sunni Islam in its Ash'arite formulation. This project became the topic of his masterpiece, *Ihya' 'ulum al-din* (The Revivification of Religious Sciences). Ghazali's work marked the period as one of theological-mystical reaction against the reason of the hellenicist philosophers, as seen in his *Tahafut al-falasifa* (The Incoherence of the Philosophers).

[5] Abu 'Ali al-Husayn Ibn Sina, the Avicenna of the Latin scholars (370-428/980-1037). He was born in Afshana in Tranoxiana (northern Iran), lived in the court of several Samanid and Iranian Buyid princes and died in Hamadan. He was the greatest name of neo-platonist Islamic philosophy and of medieval medicine. He had Farabi as a master to whom he owed his understanding of Aristotle's *Metaphysics*. His major treaty of philosophy is *Kitab al-Shifa'* (The Book of Healing). It is an encyclopedia of Greco-Islamic knowledge in the fifth/eleventh century, covering anything from logic to mathematics. Avicenna himself wrote a summary of this book which he called *Kitab al-Najat* (The Book of Salvation). His great *Al-Qanun fi al-Tibb* (The Canon of Medicine) remained the basis of medical studies

in the West for centuries and in the East practically to this day. His other major work *Kitab al-'Isharat wa al-Tanbihat* (The Book of Remarks and Admonitions) inaugurated a gnostic-"illuminist" trend in Islamic philosophical thinking.

[6] Abu al-Walid Muhammad Ibn Ahmad Ibn Muhammad Ibn Rushd (the Averroes of the Latins). He was born in Cordoba in 520/1126, a descendant of a long line of prominent jurists in Muslim Spain. He received a complete training in theology, law, medicine, mathematics, astronomy and philosophy. In 565/1169, at the initiative of the Almohad caliph Abu Ya'qub Yusuf, he started a series of commentaries on the work of Aristotle. In 578/1182, he became personal physician to the Caliph and Qadi of Cordoba. He later enjoyed the same favors with the Caliph's successor, Abu Yusuf Ya'qub al-Mansur. But his philosophical opinions drew skepticism from the legal scholars. He fell in disgrace; his books were burned and had to suffer attacks from the theologians of the populace. He died in Morocco in 595/1198 after being finally pardoned by the Almohad caliph. The three major areas in Averroes' thought were (i) his commentaries and his interpretation of Aristotle; (ii) his criticism of Farabi and Avicenna which called for an Aristotelianism free of the misinterpretations that had been inflicted on it by the Eastern philosophical tradition; and (iii) his proof of the essential agreement between philosophy and revelation as two distinct expressions of one and the same truth. With the revival of Aristotle's thinking (Aristotelianism) in Western Europe at the end of the twelfth century, he was soon hailed as a major authority in Jewish and Christian thinking.

[7] Abu Nasr Muhammad Ibn Muhammad Ibn Turkhan al-Farrabi, the Abunaser of the Latins (died 339/950). Originally from Farab in Transoxiania (northernmost of Iran), he grew up in Damascus where, according to traditional biographies, he devoted himself to reading philosophical books while working as a garden-keeper. He then went to Baghdad where he followed the teachings of two prominent logicians, Mata Ibn Yunus and Yuhanna Ibn Haylan. He then lived in Aleppo, in northern Syria, in the court of the Hamdanid Sayf al-Dawla (cf. footnote 5 in Chapter 4) and died in Damascus. He was nicknamed *al-Mu'allim al-thani* (*magister secundus*) because he exposed the science of logic founded by Aristotle, the *magister primus*, then commented and wrote treaties on it while logic, before him, was nothing but translations from Greek. His *Ihsa' al-'ulum* (The Enumeration of Sciences) was to contribute to determining a durable conception of the relationship between philosophy and the other sciences and the relationship between the Greek sciences and the Islamic sciences. He is the author of a voluminous philosophical work where he clearly expressed the will to integrate Aristotelian thinking into a neo-platonist, emanacionist, world vision, as is seen in his *Jam' bayna ra'yay al-Hakimayn* (Accord between the Opinions of the Two Sages), in which he

attempts to reconcile the spiritualist philosophy of the "divine" Plato with the Aristotelian concepts of the forms that are inherent in matter, by citing the so-called Aristotle's theology (cf. footnote 12 from chapter 5). In his political-metaphysical treaty called *The Opinions of the Virtuous City's Inhabitants*, he tries to give credit to the idea of a unifying force, ideally of a prophetic nature, but in fact reserved for sages, and founded on reason.

[8] A distinguished man from the second/eighth century whose historical existence was contested by some orientalists. A large corpus of hermetist alchemy is credited to his name. He was known to the Latins as Geber. He was the supposed disciple of the Imam Ja'far al-Sadiq, in whose circle he was supposed to have been initiated to the "esoteric" sciences. He is said to have lived a while in Harun al-Rashid's court and died around 200/815, under the reign of al-Ma'mun.

[9] Cf. footnote 20.

[10] An Egyptian journalist and man of letters (1865-1908). He was a disciple of Muhammad 'Abdu and became famous for his positions in favor of women's emancipation.

[11] A rationalist school of dialectical theology (*kalam*) that expressed the official doctrine of the Abbassid state from 211/827 to 232/847. The Mu'tazilite thinking revolved around the questions of (divine) oneness and justice. By developing the idea of absolute transcendence of God in relationship to the world, they opened a larger forum for the interpretation of the text by reason and asserted the notion of responsibility of man for his own acts. At that time, the Mu'tazilite attitude reflected the aspirations of an enlightened élite vs the attitude of the traditionalist majority, represented by the person of Ibn Hanbal, the great hadith scholar.

[12] Cf. note 5.

[13] Muhammad Ibn 'Abd al-Karim al-Shahrastani (469-548/1076-1153) was born in the city of Sharastan in Khurasan (eastern Iran). He was an Ash'arite theologian mostly known for his *kitab al-Milal wa al-Nihal* ("Book of Religions and Sects") which was a classic work in doxology generally recognized for its precision and rigor. The author surveys all the religious and philosophical systems that he knew by classifying them according to their relative remoteness from Islamic (Ash'arite) "orthodoxy," from the Mu'tazilite to the Hindu beliefs by way of the Shi'ites, the Batinists, the "people of the Book", etc.

[14] Ernest Renan (1823-1892) was a French writer, thinker, Semiticist and philologist. He devoted himself to researching the history and origins of religions (Jewish and Christian) from the perspective of understanding the religious phenomenon through a philological approach. He is the author of a work entitled : *Averroes and Averroism*. His assessment of the Arab-Islamic intellectual output is founded on a racial theory that opposes the Semitic genius , mythical and religious, to the Aryan

genius, rational and scientific. According to him, philosophical thinking by the "Semites" could only be a sterile imitation of Greek thought.

[15] A German orientalist who authored a history of Islamic philosophy that appeared in 1901 under the title *Geschichte der Philosophie im Islam*. This book is the first synthesis of the history of Islamic thought written in modern times. It was translated into Arabic and annotated by M. A. Abu Rida in 1938 and became an ongoing reference for numerous Arab academicians.

[16] Muhammad Ibn Musa al-Khawarizmi was born around 184/800 and died 232/847. A mathematician and an astronomer, originally from Khawarism, Iran, he was one of the scholars who were called to Baghdad by the Caliph al-Mamun. He is the author of the *Astronomy Tables* which were translated into Latin. He is mostly known as an algebra theoretician because of his *al-Maqala fi Hisab al-Jabr wa al-Muqabala* which was translated into Latin in the twelfth century under the title of *Liber Algebrae et Amucabola.*

[17] Abu Bakr a-Karkhi (also al-Karaji), who died after 409/1019, was one of Baghdad's mathematicians and the author of books on algebra and arithmetic, e.g., *al-Kafi fi al-Hisab*, which was a compendium of arithmetic, algebra, and cadastre.

[18] Samaw'al Ibn Yahya al-Maghribi (died around 570/1174) was a Jewish logician, mathematician, and physician with origins in the Maghreb. He resided in Baghdad and converted to Islam. He is also the author of a treatise on medicine called *al-Mufid al-Awsat* and of various books on geometry.

[19] Abu 'Abdallah Muhammad al-Battani, known to Latin scholars as Albategnius (244-317/858-929), was an astronomer of Harranian origins. He lived in Raqqa (northern Syria). His family practiced the Sabean religion (cf. note 27, Chapter 5). He is the author of a book on astronomy called *Al-Zijj* (A Treatise and Tables in Astronomy).

[20] Abu Bakr Muhammad Ibn Zakariyya' al-Rhazi, known to the Latin scholars as Rhazes (236-313/850-925), is sometimes mistaken for his homonyms: Fakhr al-Din al-Rhazi, a sixth/twelfth-century theologian and philosopher and Qutb al-Din al-Rhazi, an eighth/fourteenth-century Avicennian illuminist thinker. Rhazes was a renown physician and a philosopher of Pythagorean-leaning who defended some very bold theses. He was the hospital director of his native Rayy (a city south of present-day Teheran), then later held a similar position in Baghdad. His greatest medical work *Al-Hawi,* also known as *Al-jami',* or compendium of medicine, was translated into Latin in 1279 under the title of *Liber Continens* and was widely circulated among the medical community until the sixteenth century. His works dealt with, in addition to all aspects of medicine, philosophy, alchemy, astronomy, grammar, theology, logic and other fields of knowledge.

Chapter III
Historical Dynamics of the Arab-Islamic Philosophy

No great moment in human thought has, without doubt, been—and remains—more unfairly treated by philosophical historians than the moment of Islamic philosophy. The ancient historians and doxographers consider it like a foreign object and like a set of "imported sciences" against which they protested, and treated it like an orphan child, perhaps even like an illegitimate one. Some contemporary Arab authors, while rehashing past conflicts in their writings and while consciously or unconsciously engaging in them, continue to echo such judgment and take the same position against Islamic philosophy as the ancient theologians did, sometimes assuming the persona of a Ghazali[1], sometimes that of an Ibn Taymiyya[2], but very rarely the less partial persona of a Shahrastani. As for the orientalists and those Arab scholars who followed their path, they merely consider it as a continuation of Greek philosophy during the Hellenic era which amounts once again to making it a foreign "body" totally isolated inside the Arab-Islamic society. Some of these orientalists themselves do not hesitate to resuscitate, in their own way, the tensions amongst Medieval Arab thinkers, accusing Islamic thought of inconsistency and sterility, and taking a partial stance with theology and with Sufism. As for the leftist Arab intellectuals, their research in the end only stands out by the way it rechannels the broad outline of the theses that inspire historical materialism. They sometimes speak of class struggle, other times of "historical conspiracy," and yet other times of the struggle between "materialism" and "idealism," without ever going beyond the general framework of their preconceived schema.

Although all these positions may differ as to the origins of their inspiration or as to their goals, they ultimately lead to the same outcome: dissociating philosophical thinking in Islam from its cultural, political, social and civilization contexts, which means disfiguring its identity and its role and suppressing the true course of its evolution.

In order to de-alienate the consciousness that the Arabs have of their history, we must "put things back in place," in the very heart of this history and first rethink all those ahistorical conceptions that have been shaping Arab consciousness to this day, imposing on it a representation of its history that disseminates its coherence. The Arab-Islamic philosophy, one of the fragments of this history, is the first victim of those conceptions. Its "story" was always written outside of its own history, the one it contributed to construct. That thought which, earlier on, we asked the reader to examine as a whole, as a unity, since it does revolve around one and the same problematics, belonged itself during its heyday to a larger entity and was a component within a whole: that of the medieval Arab-Islamic society, a whole that encompasses the economic, the social, the cultural, the religious aspects, etc. We must therefore look at this philosophy within the framework of this unity and in light of its contradictions and its conflicts if we really want to write its "story" within history itself rather than within an indefinite elsewhere.

Arab-Islamic philosophy, if understood along these lines, will prove to be a militant ideological discourse that is committed to the service of science, progress and a dynamic conception of society; which means that its enemies in the past had always come from among the reactionary and conservative elements of society, often among those whose ethnic or class interests forced history to move backwards.

This phenomenon could be seen as early as the period when the first Arabic translations of the great texts from Greek philosophy had been commissioned. This work, carried out at the beginning of the Abbassid era, mostly under the reign of the Caliph al-Ma'mun,[3] was by no means an "innocent" operation or a "neutral" educational endeavor naturally flowing from the intellectual evolution of the time. Instead, it was part of a broader strategy used by the—newly established—Abbassid dynasty to confront hostile forces, namely the Persian aristocracy who, anxious for revenge, had resolved to fight on the ideological front following their failed attempts on the political and social fronts.[4]

This aristocracy, which had espoused the cause of the "descendants of the Prophet's family" (*ahl al-bayt*)[5] during their revolution against the Omeyyad State, had understood very well that power, within the Arab-Islamic society of those days, was of an ideological order. It was ideology, in this case Islam, that secured secular domination, by helping to attenuate or sublimate tribal conflicts, quell or avert social conflicts [through conquests]. This aristocracy therefore decided to go into action on the very [battle]field where the strength of the Arab State resided, the [battle]field of ideology. The weapon it chose to use was its own cultural and religious heritage based upon gnosticism, i.e., the belief in the existence of a source of knowledge other than reason, illumination, or divine inspiration that does not cease with the end of the prophecy,[6] a "continuous revelation" that does not leave any room for either reason or transmission.

The Persian aristocracy thus launched a large ideological offensive, using a religious-cultural heritage that drew its inspiration from Zoroastrianism[7], Manicheism,[8] and Mazdaism[9] in order to discredit the religion of the Arabs and undermine its foundations and thus overthrow the Arab power-state. In retaliation to these attacks, the early Abbassid state encouraged the Mu'tazilite theologians by officially adopting their doctrine, and by importing, translating and distributing scientific and philosophical works produced by the hereditary foes of the Persians (the Byzantine Greeks). Caliph al-Ma'mun's "dream," real or not, was in any case by no means innocent. It did not come about out of pure interest for Aristotle, but rather to thwart Zoroaster and Manes.

The task of the Arab-Islamic philosophy of the future was therefore clearly defined from the time when it was only a project, the time of the early translations. It had to become a weapon against the ideological offensive of gnosticism which was aimed at the very foundations of the state.

On the other hand, it was natural that the support lent to the Mu'tazilites by the Abbassid caliphs—which support was said to have been originally motivated by the necessity to resist the gnostic offensive—would provoke the wrath of the "partisans of the Prophet's Tradition" (*ahl al-sunna*), [10] opponents of the Mu'tazilites, and the rage of the literalist jurists (*fuqaha*). All of these angry opponents used their diatribes against the sciences of the "ancient ones"[11] and against philosophy as a convenient means to express a veiled opposition to the state that had sponsored the translations of scientific texts and the spread of philosophy. Philosophy was thus forced to face two indomitable enemies simultaneously: gnosticism (which later became Sufism) and the traditionalist jurists. The gnostics realized that their theses could very easily be sullied and discredited by the Mu'tazilites' dialectical logic. This logic was based on the reasoning method that establishes the legitimacy of the knowledge of an *in absentia* element, the object-to-know, from an *in praesentia* element that can be observed in the world of empirical data. Any knowledge that is based on illumination[12] could not compete with such [reasoning] method. Consequently, the gnostics, aware of the superiority that their opponents alone had in the area of "ancient sciences," once again shielded themselves behind Shi'ism and, this time, succeeded in using it to their ideological advantage. They, in turn, resorted to the "sciences of the ancient ones" (particularly the magical sciences) and used them in the Shi'ite thought under whose cover they were now working. It was from this that Isma'ilism[13] and the *Epistles of the Brothers of Purity*[14] had emerged. Now, the two opponents were holding the same weapon in hand and as a result, the "partisans of tradition" were able to stand as a third force, the alternative as it were. This explains the "coup d'etat"—against the Mu'tazilites—under the caliphate of al-Mutawakkil.[15] Hence, the debate began to form around the opposition between partisans of "transmission" and partisans of "reason," between the reactionary and conservative forces that held the power and the opposition forces represented by society's upwardly mobile strata who aspired to a state built on reason, brotherhood and justice. It was philosophy which helped articulate this debate.

---

[1] Cf. note 4 of Chapter II

[2] Taqiy al-Din Ahmad Ibn Taymiyya (661-728/1263-1328) was born in Harran (northern Mesopotamia) and died in prison in Damascus. He was a major figure of the Hanbalite traditionalist theology and therefore a most vehement opponent to the philosophers' position. He is the author of *al-Radd 'ala al-mantiqiyyin* (Refutation of the Logicians), which spoke against the abuses of philosophy and theology and against the major theses of the great philosophers (Farabi, Avicenna), while advocating a return to the ancient scholars' (*salaf*) orthodox methods. He became famous for his virulent criticism of Shi'ism and of Sufism (Ibn 'Arabi). A few centuries later, he inspired what they called the modern Hanbalite renewal, namely the Wahhabite movement in the eighteenth century, then the Salafite fundamentalist reform in the nineteenth century.

[3] He was the seventh Abbassid caliph (198-218/813-833), son of Harun al-Rashid and of a Persian concubine. In 211/827, he proclaimed Mu'tazilism (cf. note 11 of chapter 2) as state doctrine and thus became at odds with the traditionalist circles. He founded a prestigious scientific institution, called the House of Wisdom (*Bayt al-Hikma*), to push for the translation and the distribution of Greek science texts.

[4] The ancient Arab scholars report that Caliph al-Ma'mun had presumably commissioned the translation of Aristotle's works after seeing the latter in a dream. This story is reported by Ibn al-Nadiim (died 385/995), author of *The Fihrist* (The Catalogue), as follows: Caliph al-Ma'mun saw, in his dream, a light-skin,

red-faced man, with a wide forehead and conjoined eyebrows. He was bald with dark-blue eyes, had friendly manners and was sitting in a chair. "I was," said al-Ma'mun, "almost touching him, so to speak, and that made me feel a great fear. I asked him: 'Who are you?' 'I am Aristotle,' he answered. This made me rejoice so I told him: 'Oh wise one I am going to ask you something.' He said: 'Ask.' I told him: 'What is good?' 'What is good according to reason,' he answered. I told him: 'And after?' 'What is good according to the revelation,' he answered. I told him: 'And after?' 'What is good in the eyes of all,' he answered. I told him: 'And after?' ·'After, there is no after,' he answered." (Ibn al-Nadiim, *Kitab al-Fihrist*, ed. Flügel, p. 343).

M. A. al-Jabri notes that Aristotle's answers come in appropriately handy in support of the Mu'tazilites' position: [that] reason is first, then [comes] the revelation, then [comes] collective opinion. As for the sentence "after, there is no after," it means that there is no other access to knowledge. This is a clear refutation of gnostism and illuminism. This dream is therefore aimed at the gnostism of the Manicheans...

[5] The expression "descendants of the Prophet's family" or "people of the House" *(ahl al-bayt)* refers to the descendance of 'Ali Ibn Abi Talib, cousin and son-in-law of the Prophet Muhammad and that of Fatima, daughter of the Prophet. A wing of this political-religious opposition to the Omeyyad rule, having taken shape around the claim to the "Imamate" by members of this lineage, is at the origin of the Shi'ite branch of Islam. During the period that preceded the Abbassid revolt against the Omeyyad rule in Damascus, feelings of loyalty to the Prophet's descendants began to spread in Iran by way of secret propagandists *(da'i)* coming from Iraq. Several networks of diverse persuasions had become involved in this action which was the work of a revolutionary movement and which gave hopes to pretenders to various titles, ranging from 'Ali's descendants to those of Al-'Abbas, the Prophet's uncle. It was the latter who, after ousting 'Ali's followers, founded the Abbassid's dynasty.

[6] In the Islamic tradition, the Qur'anic revelation is designated as the last of all revelations sent by God to humans and the prophet Muhammad is referred to as the "seal of prophets."

[7] Ancient religion of Iran, born of a reform of Indo-Iranian Mazdaism. It was the official religion during the Sassanid era before the Islamic conquest. Its origins go back to around 700 or 800 B.C. and its founder, Zoroaster (Zarathustra), is the author of the *Gatha* hymns that were subsequently included in the Zoroastrian holy book, the (Zend) *Avesta*. His teachings influenced some of the later religions, namely his doctrine of *post mortem* resurrection, the existence of the soul, of Heaven and Hell, the end of times and of the world following a battle between the forces

of good and those of evil and the belief in a universal doomsday. The Koran calls Zoroastrians *Majus*. From the time of 'Umar Ibn al-Khattab's caliphate on, the Muslim authorities recognized the status of Zoroastrians as "People of the Book" (*ahl al-kitab*), endowed with a revealed religion. Their status was that of tributaries (*dhimmis*) and were thus not forced to embrace Islam.

[8] The religion of Manes, a Persian prophet who was born in 216 A.D. He was originally from Mesopotamia and was raised among a "Baptist" Judeo-Christian sect; and just before the Sassanid Persian empire was established, he founded his own religion. Manes was backed by the early Sassanid leaders who saw in his "syncretist" doctrine a potential support for their imperial and supranational rule, but he later had to face a reactionary movement by the Mazdean clergy who accused supporters of Manes of being heretics (*zindiqs*). Manes was imprisoned and, according to his followers, probably "made-martyr" in 277. Manes' doctrine purported to be the inner and secret truth of all religions. It encompassed elements from Christianity, from Zoroastrianism, from Greek paganism, from Budhism and from Taoism. It was based on the principle of duality which considers that good and evil are both active poles of the same reality, both possessing an essence and a reality that is independent from the other one's reality. The Manichean cosmology calls for the idea of a creation by emanation of the "good God" in the darkness. Light and darkness coexist in the world, and man's salvation consists in safeguarding the light that is buried within him. Manicheism survived as a belief and as a highly structured "clandestine" organization. It became a real threat to Muslim rule at the beginning of the Abbassid era when it was considered as *zandaqa* (nonbelief) and was combatted.

[9] The religion of Mazdak (sixth century A.D.), a Mazdean priest who became a dissident from the Zoroastrian orthodoxy. He preached the communal sharing of women and wealth as well as duality like Manes. The Persian Emperor Kavadh, known to the Arabs as Qubadh (488-531), first adhered to this form of worship but ended up being convinced of its unorthodox character. Mazdak and his followers were put to death by Khosraw Anusharvan.

[10] That is to say the traditionalists who asserted the primacy of tradition over reason. This trend was represented by masters like Ibn Hanbal (died 241/855), who was persecuted under al-Ma'mun's reign for having refused to subscribe to the Mu'tazilite thesis of the created Koran.

[11] *'Ulum al-'awa'il* or *'Ulum al-'aqdamin*. The Muslims of those days used these terms to refer to the sciences (i.e., philosophy, medicine, mathematics, astrology etc.) inherited from ancient civilizations (e.g., Greek, Persian, Indian, etc.).

[12] Regarding the notions of "indication" (*bayan*), "demonstration" (*burhan*) and "illumination" (*'irfan*) as used by M.A. al-Jabri.

[13] It is an offshoot of Shi'ism born from the split that occurred following the death of al-Sadiq (died 148/765), the sixth "imam" in Ali's lineage who had designated his son Isma'il as successor. But Isma'il prematurely died before his father. Consequently, al-Sadiq, shortly before his own death, had re-assigned his succession to one of his other children, Musa al-Kadhim. A group of disciples, who were especially drawn to the esoteric scientific work of Imam Ja'far, had formed around Imam Isma'il. This group gave birth to the seven-imam system within the Isma'ilian Shi'ism. The majority of Shi'ites, who recognize the legitimacy of Musa al-Kadhim and his descendants up to the twelfth imam ("disappeared" in 329/940 and "expected" at the end of times), represent the twelve-imam system in Shi'ism.

[14] These were scientific and philosophical texts that came out around the time of the Buyid protectorate in Iraq (fourth/tenth century). They were thought to have been written by the "Brothers of Purity" (*Ikhwan al-Safa*), a philosophical-religious society from Basra. This group had sprung from among those Isma'ilians who had dedicated themselves to secret propaganda from around 148/765. These epistles, a kind of Shi'ite propagandist encyclopedia, were divided in four types: mathematics, physics, psychological-intellectual and theological-juridical. The philosophical vision of the "Brothers" shows a neo-platonist emanationist character with a pronounced neo-Pythagoreanism. Some sources attribute the writing of the *Epistles* to a descendant of "Imam" Isma'il who may have lived during the period of "occultation" in the Isma'ilian lineage. He is said to have written the texts to counter al-Ma'mun, his Abbassid contemporary, who used Greek sciences in the service of his political-religious project. According to this hypothesis, the Epistles go back to the third/ninth century.

[15] This caliph, who ruled from 232/847-247/861, reversed his uncle al-Ma'mun's religious policy. He used the tradionalists' help to strengthen his rule and in return freed Ibn Hanbal, their spiritual leader (cf. note 10) and persecuted the Mu'tazilites.

Chapter IV
The Rise and Fall of Reason

Philosophy was never an intellectual luxury within Islamic society. It was in fact, ever since its birth, a militant ideological discourse. Al Kindi,[1] the first Muslim philosopher, was directly involved in the ideological conflict that existed during his lifetime between the Mu'tazilites, then representing the state's ideology, on the one hand and the gnostics and the "Sunnites" on the other. Al-Kindi fought on two fronts: (1) against the gnostics, by publishing summaries of the lectures he gave, within the area of rational sciences, in the form of concise installments (epistles) and a simplified reading, designed to spread among the wider public and among the elite of the Arab readership certain rationalist concepts of man and the universe, while respecting the constants of Islamic[2] religious thinking; and (2) against the rigorist legal scholars, whom he described as "those who went astray from the truth," those who declared their hostility to philosophy "out of fear of losing the positions they have undeservedly usurped, out of a taste for power, and who commodify religion and (thus) have no religion—for he who trades in something, soon sells it and does not own it any longer. Therefore, he who commodifies religion no longer has a religion, and he who refuses to acquire knowledge of the truth about things and denounces it as impiety (*kufr*) deserves to lose his title of 'religious'..." Al-Kindi stated that there existed a parallelism between religion and philosophy and believed that the two were in agreement and in harmony and that both aimed at one thing: knowledge of the "true," of God's truth, of nature and of man: "The sayings of Muhammad, the truthful—may the prayers of God be upon him— as well as the word that was dictated to him by God—may His power and His might be witnessed, all of which can be grasped through reasoning that is only refuted by those men who are deprived of rationality, those who are hand in glove together with ignorance."

Al-Kindi was therefore the initiator of the research on "Arabization" and on the acclimatization of philosophy to the Arab cultural space. Thanks to his work, the cognitive material borrowed from "the sciences of the ancient ones" was re-invested within the ideological conflict that opposed the enlightened thinkers of the Arab-Islamic society of his era to reactionary and conservative forces. These forces had, in turn, called for a new appropriation of both gnosticism (Sufism) and literalism (juridical but not theological) despite the difficulty of conciliating two such incompatible trends.

Al-Farabi[3] came a few decades later. In the meantime, there occurred the famous Sunnite "coup d'etat" against the Mu'tazilites. This was the height of the period of strikes by the Shi'ite dynasties, e.g., the Buyids[4] and the Hamdanids,[5] against a caliphate that had turned into a merely nominal institution. Thus began the break up of the Arab Empire into competing and adversary small states. The ideological debate became divided with the multiplication of doctrines and sects, something that threatened both the unity of the regime and the permanence of the state, and consequently the unity of thought and the permanence of society. Therefore, in all of al-Farabi's works there was a call on this thought and this society to restore their unity. To restore the unity of thought meant to go beyond the rationalist, segmentarist-atomist, discourse of the Mu'tazilites, which had failed to conciliate between reason and transmission, by adopting the discourse of the "universal reason" according to which religion and philosophy differ from one another only in their medium of expression. The former resorts to dialectical and rhetorical processes, the latter to the demonstrative method. This is why their opposition is reducible if we consider that "what religion says is the allegory of what philosophy says." To restore the unity of society meant to establish social relationships on the model of harmony and of the pyramidal hierarchy that prevail in the universe.

When reading al-Farabi's political and religious philosophy within this perspective, one discovers a thinker quite different from the image usually reflected of him in history textbooks. Al-Farabi was not an isolated man who was cut off from the world, as he sat meditating under the shade of trees in some garden in the outskirts of Damascus, but a man who was concerned about the problems of the society in which he lived. He assumed the preoccupations of his contemporaries and was not at all desperate, afflicted or tired of living. He was an optimist who believed in progress and in solving problems through reason, and it was this faith that motivated his dream of the "virtuous city," a city of reason, of harmony, of fraternity and of justice in which he invested all the sciences of his era, especially the rational sciences.

Al-Farabi's thought was an ideological project that placed philosophy and the philosophical sciences at the service of a given cause. It was perhaps the project of an idealist and even of a dreamer. But it was also a militant rationalist discourse, to the point where it would not be too farfetched to wonder if al-Farabi was not, in the Middle Ages, the Rousseau of the Arabs.

It would not have been normal, or even conceivable that Avicenna, al-Farabi's successor, would want to resuscitate the dream of a worldly virtuous city built essentially on reason, he who had lived in an era when the dismemberment of the Arab Empire had reached its worst. He who had resided in Iran-based princedoms that were zealous patrons of the Persian culture, in an intellectual climate characterized by rivalries between the "Easterners," his Khurasanian compatriots, and the "Westerners," the Iraqis, the Syrians and other even more Western hereditary enemies; and he who, as vizier to the Buyid sovereign, had personally experienced a real city, plagued by so much confusion and by so many political, social, economic and cultural disturbances.

If Avicenna indeed adopted al-Farabi's emanationist[6] scheme, it was not to apply it to society or to history, even in the form of a dream, but was somewhat like a ladder that would allow him access to the heavens, so he could reserve from this world a place for his soul in the afterlife.

This other side to the "great master"[7] appears in his "Eastern philosophy,"[8] which he considers as "the truth that is not blemished by any impurity." We must show Avicenna's gnostic side which promotes gloom-thinking in order to get used to reading our past in light of objective data and no longer under the pressure of our present *desiderata*. We must not be afraid of facing this dark side of Avicenna's thought which contradicts the other side, the one that reflects his great work *Al-Shifa'*. Our tradition does not enjoy the exclusivity of such contradictions; even today, at the dawn of the twenty-first century, they are legal tender in the Arab world and elsewhere.

Nevertheless, one could say that Avicenna, even with his Eastern philosophy—the philosophy of the "other life" (in this world and in the next world)— was a man who was engaged in the conflicts of his time, a militant for one cause. This philosophy, which he qualified as being "Eastern" albeit an irrationalist discourse, was also an ideological discourse which, given its subsequent developments, proved to be a project of national (Persian) philosophy. What is of importance to us is not the discourse in itself, nor its motivations, but rather its consequences. With his Eastern philosophy, Avicenna consecrated a spiritualist and gnostic trend whose impact was instrumental in the regression of Arab thinking from an open rationalism, spearheaded by the Mu'tazilites, then by al-Kindi, and culminating with al-Farabi, to a pernicious irrationalism which augured the "gloom-thinking" that scholars like Ghazali, Suhrawardi of Aleppo,[9] and others simply spread and popularized in various circles. Such is my judgment against Avicenna, the illustrious philosopher and physician that the Eastern school of philosophy had produced. It is without hesitation and regardless of current ideas that I am formulating it, because I believe that it is history itself that judges him as such, history as it actually happened, not textbook "history."

As a thinker, Avicenna had two sides to him: the side reflected in his *Kitab al-Shifa'* or his *Kitab al-Najat*, and the side that appears in his *Kitab al-'Isharat wa al-Tanbihat* and in the "Eastern" Epistles. Thus through an irony of fate, critics have always used Avicenna to censure Avicenna. Ghazali accepted responsibility for the contents of Avicenna's Eastern philosophy which he presented as the "Deliverance from Bewilderment"[10] and as the "Revivification of Religious Sciences."[11] It is in the name of this Eastern philosophy and in the name of religion that he examined the case against Avicenna. The echoes of the sentence that he rendered were to resound for a long time in the decrees of the rigorist legal scholars. Ghazali and those who imitated him made of Avicenna the official representative of philosophy in Islam, by referring to two of his works, the *Shifa'* and the *Najat*, but concealing the *Kitab al-'Isharat wa al-Tanbihat* and "the Eastern wisdom." They brought action against philosophy in his person and accused him of hostility to a cause to which he had in fact adhered but which he could not easily defend during his time because he had borrowed the theologians' methods. Following his death, these very opponents took his place in defending his cause, that of the "Eastern" philosophy, exposing "the intentions of philosophers," denouncing "the incoherence of philosophers" and engaging in the "struggle against philosophers."[12] That was the best of their talents.

If indeed—as it has constantly been reiterated—philosophy never was able to recover from the blows dealt to it by Ghazali, this was only true in the case of the Arab Middle East. In Iran, by contrast, the Avicennian tradition lasted and its prolongation remained alive until today, expressing, in Persian, a kind of national identity, as this thought was taken out of the sphere of the Arab-Islamic philosophy and placed in that of the Iranian illuminist philosophy.

But let us leave Iran aside and turn our attention towards the Muslim West to discover an Arab-Islamic philosophy (mostly based in the Maghreb and in Al-Andalus), which developed its own problematics after breaking with the problematics of the Easterners. It is inside the Muslim West that philosophy continued its struggle for reason and rationality, this time addressing the problem through a new methodology and within new perspectives.

---

[1] Abu Yusuf Ya'qub Ibn Ishaq al-Kindi (185-269/796-873) was descended from the great South Arabian tribe of Kinda, a fact that earned him the honorific title of "Philosopher of the Arabs." He was born in Kufa when his father was governor of that city. He studied in Basra, then a great intellectual center, and later settled down in Baghdad. There, he enjoyed the sponsorship of caliphs: al-Ma'mun, al-Mu'tasim (218-227/833-842) and al-Wathiq (227-232/842-847), but was subsequently persecuted under the reign of al-Mutuwakkil. Through his logic, metaphysics, arithmetic, medicine, theology, etc., he contributed greatly to the acclimatization of Greek sciences to Islamic thought. Several of his philosophical treatises were translated into Latin and became famous in the West during the Middle Ages. His thought is heavily influenced by Aristotle as we can judge from his *Treaty of the Original Philosophy*, among others.

[2] One of the major points of dichotomy between Greek thought and [Islamic] religious thought was the problem of the *ex nihilo* creation or the eternity of the world. Al-Kindi was convinced of the fundamental agreement between research in rational philosophy and the prophetic revelation, but thought that each one represented a distinct path towards the truth. While remaining close to theology, he defended the thesis of the *ex nihilo* creation.

[3] See note 7, Chapter 2.

[4] A dynasty of Iranian Shi'ite princes originally from Daylam (Northern Iran), founded in 300/913. Taking advantage of the political unrest and the potential collapse that threatened the caliphate in Baghdad, it succeeded in imposing a sort of protectorate on the latter in 334/945. This regime was to last until 447/1055. Despite their Shi'ite persuasion, the Buyids never questioned the nominal sovereignty of the Abbassid caliphs.

[5] A dynasty of Arab princes originally from the Thaghlib tribe, two branches of which succeeded in acquiring sovereignty over the northwest part of the Abbassid Empire—one in Jazira, with Mawsul as a capital, and the other in northern Syria, with Aleppo as a capital. This second princedom knew its glory mostly between 336/947 and 350/961 under the reign of Sayf al-Dawla who fought successfully against the Byzantines and who welcomed into his court numerous thinkers and men-of-letters, like al-Mutanabbi, the poet, and al-Farabi, the philosopher.

[6] Emanationism is the theory advanced by the neo-platonists according to which spirits and bodies come onto the [human] being through a necessary outflow (*fayd*) of divine power, in the same way light emanates from the sun. This theory was invested within the Arab-Islamic philosophy by al-Farabi. In his "Opinions of the Inhabitants of the Virtuous City," he views the whole of creation as resulting from the overabundance in perfection of the one (God), which overflows into a primary intelligence that generates, in turn, a secondary intelligence, through the act of understanding its author, and the extreme celestial sphere, through the act of self-understanding. This process continues through successive stages until the tenth cosmic intelligence is generated. The various intelligences determine the movement of the celestial spheres that govern the sub-lunary world. The contribution of such a theory is to have satisfactorily answered the questions of Muslims who were faced with the problem of reconciling the rational require-ment—as posited by the Aristotelian philosophy—of a necessity that is inherent to the existence of the Universe implying the eternity of the world, with the requirement of conceiving of the world as being contingent, as postulated by the dogma of the *ex-nihilo* creation. Moreover, the theory of the procession of intel-ligences helped resolve the problem of the creation of the multiple from the one. Similarly, emanation was the object of exploration by the Shi'ite thinkers as well, in particular by Ja'far al-Sadiq who is said to have identified the primary intellect with the Prophet (the Muhammadan light) and the secondary intellect with Imam 'Ali. The articulation of "Imamology"—or hagiology—after noesis became par-ticularly systematized within the Isma'ilian thought and among the Sufis.

[7] *Shaikh ra'is*, the honorific title attributed to Avicenna by the Islamic philoso-phy tradition.

[8] In his *Kitab al-Shifa'*, Avicenna expressly refers to another work in which he is said to have presented an "Eastern philosophy" or "Eastern wisdom," that must have revealed his true doctrine. In it were gathered "the principles of true science that are discovered—through exhaustive research and prolonged reflection—by he who is not without a fine intellectual intuition." The *Shifa'* and the *Najat*, devoted to peripatetic [rationalist] philosophy, were works he therefore reserved for the commoners, whereas his spiritualist, gnostic, "Eastern philosophy" was

reserved for the elite. M. A. al-Jabri proposed an analysis of this particular question in a text entitled *Ibn Sina wa falsafatuhu al-mashriqiyy*a (Avicenna and his "Eastern Philosophy") which he included in his work *Nahnu wa al-turath* and where he suggests that Avicenna's Eastern philosophy represents a moment of "resignation of reason" within the Arab-Islamic philosophy, and the beginning of a "thought of gloom."

[9] Shihab al-Din Yahya al-Suhrawardi (549-587/1155-1191) was originally from the city of Suhraward (northeastern Iran), the same birthplace of the other Suhrawardi: Abu Hafs Shihab al-Din 'Umar al-Suhrawardi (539-632/1145-1234), the Baghdad-based "Great Shaykh" of Sufism and author of a classical Sufi treatise called *Kitab 'Awarif al-Ma'arif* ("The Benefits of Spiritual Knowledge"). Shihab al-Din Yahya, nicknamed Shaykh al-Ishraq, tried to resuscitate the unfinished project of Avicenna's "Eastern philosophy." He consummated the break with nationalism in favor of a mystic approach founded on "direct experience" of the truth, which he called "illumination" *(Ishraq)*. "Eastern" Theosophy (*Hikmat al-Ishraq*), the title of Suhrawardi's *magnum opus,* was placed under the aegis of uninterrupted chains of "enlightened" interpreters, Plato, Hermes, Pythagoras in the West, the "Ancient Sages of Persia" and Zoroaster in the East, who would rejoin together in the person of the author. Suhrawardi was thus able to integrate, through "mystical epics," themes of Iranian mythology to the religious meta-history of Islamic spirituality. He was welcomed in Aleppo by the Ayyubid sovereign, son of Salah al-Din (Saladin), but was later killed following an action brought against him by the religious scholars. The image of Suhrawardi was restored in the modern era by (the orientalist) Henry Corbin's works (see Volume II of his book *In Iranian Islam*, entitled *Suhrawardi and Persia's Platonists*).

[10] *Al-Munqid min al-Dalal:* the title of one of Ghazali's works.

[11] *Ihya' 'Ulum al-Din:* the title of Ghazali's great theological-mystical work.

[12] The phrases in between quotations are titles of works that were devoted to the refutation of philosophy. The first two, *Maqasid al-falasifa* and *Tahafut al-falasifa* are Ghazali's. The third one, *Musara'at al-falasifa,* is a work by Shahrastani.

Chapter V
The Andalusian Resurgence

Causes

In the Maghreb and in Al-Andalus, two regions that had dissociated themselves from the Abbassid Empire since its very inception and had always escaped Fatimid[1] domination, intellectual activity met with a different fate than in the East, a fact for which we can suggest two main reasons:

(1) The absence of a pre-Islamic heritage: neither Al-Andalus nor Morocco (both of which having remained linked to each other from the time of the conquest till the fall of Granada) experienced a real resurgence of belief systems from before Islam, as was the case in Syria, Iraq and to some extent in Egypt. Here, as in the whole of North Africa, the Muslim conquest eliminated (tabula-rasa style) all signs of the past. Although a great number of native Andalusians did maintain their Christian or Jewish religions, their civilization never made a significant impact on the local Arab-Islamic culture. Why? Because the Andalusian civilization before the Islamic conquest was no longer strong or flourishing enough to be able to influence that of the conquerors. Sa'id the Andalusian,[2] a famous historian from Cordoba, tracking the history of culture and thought among the nations that preceded Islam and the Islamic community both in the East and in the West, notes that Al-Andalus "of the ancient times never practiced any scientific research, and not one of its inhabitants was ever famous for having engaged in such an activity." According to the same scholar, this land "remained devoid of all wisdom until the Muslim conquest in the month of Ramadan of the year ninety-two of the hijra. Even after this date, its inhabitants limited themselves to developing the juridical and the linguistic sciences until the

advent and the strengthening of the Omeyyad government that succeeded the era of discord;[3] thereafter a number of broadminded people became inspired and sought to acquire knowledge." By noting that prior to the Islamic conquest, there existed in Al-Andalus no culture capable of competing with that of the conquerors and since the flourishing of such culture did not really begin until the Omeyyad rule became finally well-established, *Qadi* (Judge) Sa'id only confirms a historical reality that is indisputably accepted nowadays.

(2) The fact that Al-Andalus and the Maghreb had remained independent from, and ideologically in conflict with, the Abbassid caliphate and likewise with the Fatimids subsequently, thus creating a constant cultural competition.

As a matter of fact, Al-Andalus did not experience any real scientific expansion until the start of the reign of 'Abd al-Rahman III (Al-Nasir) (300-350/912-962), who succeeded in transforming the "Marwanid Emirate" of Al-Andalus into a second Omeyyad caliphate, competing with both the Abbassid and Fatimid caliphates and disputing their legitimacy. We must emphasize the fact that Al-Andalus and the Maghreb regions had, during all this period, proceeded no further than the level of intellectual activity of the time of the early conquest, i.e., Islam of the companions (*sahaba*) and the followers (*tabi'un*),[4] whose basic sources for the acquisition of knowledge remained oral accounts (*riwaya*) and transmission (*naql*), be it for religious, linguistic or other knowledge, unlike the situation in the East where one could find numerous schools of law, theology and grammar. Though some of the political or intellectual movements that were fighting each other in the East may have had their echoes resounding as far away as the Maghreb and Al-Andalus through some "propagandists" (*da'is*) or because of the West-to-East travels by pilgrims, scholars, or traders, none of them was however successful in gaining ground or predominance. They always remained marginal and little-known and when their influence managed to take root after all, it always remained limited to certain closed and clandestine circles. And so Al-Andalus and the Maghreb maintained their intellectual and doctrinal autonomy in the same way they had maintained their political independence. They remained "virgin" territory—or almost—lacking any influence other than that of the "ancient scholars' Islam" (*salaf*), that of the dogma of the "people of hadith" in its original form—preceding the birth of Ash'arism[5] — the Islam of scholarship in the *hadith* and in the companions' consultations (*fatwas*). In the early days of its existence, the newly established Omeyyad regime imposed the Awza'i[6] School as the state's official School of Law. This school, traditionally rooted in Syria, the original homeland of the Omeyyads, was not, methodologically speaking, much different from the juridical position of the first conquerors, since it also resorted to transmission and oral accounts as primary sources of the law. The Abbassids in the East had adopted the doctrine of the Hanafite[7] School (that of the Iraqis), and Malik Ibn Anas, founder of the Malikite School of Jurisprudence, was perceived as a figure of opposition to the Abbassid regime, not only because of the school's doctrine that made wide use of the Prophet's sayings—as opposed to the Hanafi'te School, which preferred personal opinion (*ra'y*)—but also because of some politically motivated positioning that he was rumored to have taken against the Abbassids. Therefore, the Omeyyad regime in Al-Andalus no longer minded the spread of this Malikite School and went as far as adopting it as the state's official School of Jurisprudence. This is how the Malikite jurists began to expand their intellectual power and to act as ideological mentors to the subjects on behalf of the Omeyyad regime of Al-Andalus.

The authority of the jurists in the field of knowledge and education

In order not to lightly attribute some ready-made qualifiers to these jurists, such as "rigorism," and in order not to accuse them of being responsible for "the stifling of freedom of thought," we ought to reiterate the importance of the ideological factor in Islamic societies, both in the East and in the West. The ideological weapon is therefore one of the most dreaded weapons, if not the most dreaded. Both the regime and the opposition avidly vie for its appropriation and for its most efficient manipulation. The ideological hold and the intellectual hegemony constitute privileged means of access to secular domination. The Malikite jurists, who were the ideologues of the Omeyyad State, violently opposed the other schools of jurisprudence. They opposed also the dogmatic theological and philosophical movements from the East, either through the usual cultural exchanges—which were never interrupted—or brought in by some political propagandists working for the Abbassid state, or against it and working for the splinter Shi'ite group and for the Batinid[8] esoteric groups. If our jurists were vigilantly standing guard against the intruders, it was because they were fulfilling a perfectly legitimate and necessary mission in the eyes of the "state logic," a mission of protection and self-defense. Moreover, if we were to remind ourselves that the Mosque, and in particular the Great Mosque in the Muslim world of those days, far from being simply a place of worship, was also a center for teaching and for intellectual and political propaganda, we would readily understand why our jurists had proscribed the teaching of certain disciplines in the mosque, a space shared by the "common folks." We would understand their position even better if we considered that the kind of knowledge that the jurists repressed most severely was "philosophy," not as we understand it today, but that philosophy that was entirely subordinated to ideology, the Batinid philosophy in its emanationist[9] and its Sufi illuminist forms. The knowledge that was proscribed by the Andalusian jurists under the appellation of philosophy was in fact the "scientific" substance of the opponents' ideology, i.e., the emanationist philosophy with traces of alchemy.

Our nuanced view of the attitude of the Andalusian jurists towards "philosophy" is not meant to vindicate them. We want nothing more than to look at it from the point of view of its historical consequences, those consequences "meant" by history. The jurists, most likely, had neither wanted nor foreseen those consequences. But the fact remains that the repression against the Eastern theological and philosophical movements helped protect theoretical thinking in Al-Andalus, particularly in Cordoba, the capital of the caliphate, against the simultaneous influences of the theological problematics and of the illuminist (gnostic) contagion. The scholars then took to the study of those "ancient sciences" tolerated by the jurists: e.g., mathematics, astronomy and later logic, and mastered these before the lifting of the embargo on philosophy, which was understood to be a metaphysical science. This fact was documented by the Andalusian philosopher Ibn Tufayl[10] who wrote in the introduction to his epistle *Hayy Ibn Yaqdhan*: "The people of superior minds who grew up in Al-Andalus before the spread in this land of the sciences of logic and philosophy devoted their lives to the mathematical sciences in which they reached a high level. After them, came a generation of men who, in addition, possessed rudiments of logic; they studied this discipline, which did not lead them to real perfection (...). After them came another generation of men who were more skillful in theory and who came closer to the truth." As for the historian Sa'id the Andalusian, he dates his compatriots' initial interest in the ancient sciences (mathematics, astronomy and medicine) to around the middle of the third century of the hijra, i.e., about one hundred years after the founding of the Omeyyad Emirate. He dates their initial interest in philosophy per se to the middle of the fourth century (hijra), the time when "Prince al-Hakam (al-Mustansir bi-Allah), son of 'Abd al-Rahman III (al-nasir li-Din Allah) became, during his father's life, interested in the sciences, promoted scholars, imported the major sources from the prestigious books and extraordinary texts on ancient and modern sciences, from Baghdad, Egypt, and other Eastern lands and, throughout the remainder of his father's reign, then under his own reign, gathered a more prodigious quantity of books than the Abbassids had amassed over several centuries. During his time, scholars became active and began to read the books of the ancient scholars and to learn their doctrines."

The major support for science during the time of 'Abd al-Rahman al-Nasir is by no means due to chance. It was in fact a question of breaking the siege held by the jurists, the state's ideologues, around certain proscribed and repressed disciplines. We need to consider this event, which was not without consequences, like an event from which we indeed expected these consequences. There was a desire to usher in a cultural strategy that was an integral part of the global policy by 'Abd al-Rahman III, eighth ruler of Spain's Omeyyad dynasty, who, after having ended internal strife and warded off external (Christian) threats, proclaimed himself caliph with the name of 'Abd al-Rahman al-Nasir in 316/928. The enemy of the Omeyyad State no longer was exclusively the internal opposition or the Christian enemy. After acquiring the rank of caliph, 'Abd al-Rahman prepared to confront the Abbassid and the Fatimid caliphates on the very ground where these two states confronted each other and confronted the Omeyyad state: that of ideology. It was thus imperative that he set himself off ideologically. How else could it be otherwise at a time when ideology was master? It was the time when the Isma'ilian dynasty managed to found a state and establish its Shi'ite and Fatimid caliphate; the time when Abu al-Hasan al-Ash'ari,[11] rebelling against his Mu'tazilite masters, espoused the views of the scholars of "the hadith and the community" and managed to give them a theoretical basis to the point that he ended up lending his name to a new school that was to become the official school of the Abbassid Caliphate. It became therefore imperative to give free rein to philosophy. Political and ideological necessity thus called for the creation of an Andalusian cultural agenda capable of representing a historical alternative to the Abbassid and Fatimid agendas. The caliphate institution is not only an "extension of the Prophecy for what pertains to the conduct of temporal matters," but also and especially "for what relates to the maintenance of religion." The caliphate is not only a political power but also a cultural power. Since the Abbassids and the Fatimids had both founded their cultural power upon the re-investment of a cultural heritage dating from before Islam, why would the new Omeyyad Caliphate not follow suit, with similar objectives? They had to give free rein to philosophy. This is why theoretical thinking in Al-Andalus was lucky to encounter philosophy in its [hey] day, after scholars became solidly grounded in the knowledge of mathematics, astronomy, medicine and logic, in other words all the disciplines that were at the root of philosophical thinking in Greece where they had paved the way to the only "true" philosophy, that of Aristotle, the *Magister Primus.*

It follows from the preceding remarks that the birth of philosophy in Al-Andalus came about in circumstances that were totally different from those in which it was born in the Islamic East. In the East, it was the abstruse theosophy used by the Shi'ites that appeared first. Then came Aristotle's metaphysics (both the authentic one and the so-called *Theology of Aristotle*[12]) to which the Abbassids resorted (al-Ma'mun's dream, the house of wisdom, the translations) and used as a weapon to confront the Shi'ites for cultural domination and to provide the conceptual material to their theologians. This approach did not require going through the phase of mathematics and the physical sciences and rushed development of the thought directly towards metaphysics. In Al-Andalus, however, things ran their natural course: philosophy developed there when scholars turned earnestly to the study of mathematics, astronomy, and logic for a whole century, without ever getting involved in the theologians' problematics of the conciliation between "reason" and "transmission" that was at the center of theoretical thought in the East. The Andalusian philosophers had no problem breaking free from the cultural obstacles that had restrained philosophy in the East from the start, and on which it had always remained so dependent that they ended up being integral parts of it by becoming a fundamental element of its structure: the epistemological obstacles from dialectical theology (*kalam*) and from the gnostic core of the Eastern neo-platonism. By breaking free from dialectical theology, the philosophical discourse in Al-Andalus, unlike that in the East, never fell into the rut of the problematics of reconciling "reason" and "transmission," philosophy and religion. Similarly, by breaking free from neo-platonism in its gnostic "Eastern version," it was able to dissociate itself from that movement within the Eastern philosophical school which used science to integrate religion into philosophy and philosophy into religion. Thus, science became, as with Aristotle, the sole foundation upon which philosophy built its structure. We can explain to ourselves how Averroes,[13] Cordoba's philosopher, was able to grasp Aristotle and become his greatest commentator as follows: he grew up in an intellectual milieu which, thanks to the Jurists' "rigorism" or rather thanks to the state's ideology, did not have to deal with Aristotle's "metaphysics" until he had assimilated, in depth, the founding scientific disciplines of this metaphysics: i.e., mathematics, physics and logic.

But the authentic mastery that Averroes was able to grasp from the thought of the real Aristotle was, in itself, the highest point in the revival movement of theoretical thinking in Al-Andalus, the same thought that had been adopted by the Cordobans since the time of 'Abd al-Rahman III and of his son al-Hakam, the Ma'mun of Spain's Omeyyads. I shall describe some of the aspects of this phenomenon in the following sections.

Epistemological Foundations of Theoretical Thinking in Al-Andalus

When we speak of theoretical thinking in Al-Andalus, we mean that school of thought which seemed solidly established as early as the end of the Omeyyad rule, and which discretely survived throughout the rule of the Almoravids,[14] and later re-emerged publicly during the time of the Almohads.[15] The Almohads promoted its theoretical orientations, spread it, and plotted their ideological project around it. As we have already shown, this school owes its existence to the scientific movement that was triggered by 'Abd al-Rahman III, under the sponsorship of his son al-Hakam al-Mustansir. If the cultural project that emanated from the global strategy that had inspired this scientific movement did not actually surface until a century later, more specifically with Ibn Hazm,[16] it was because the founding initiatives—in the domain of culture and thought—took shape generally at a later time, technically two generations at least after their birth, and then only much later did they bear any fruit. This is because any new structure that wants to be established within a given cultural system never does so upon virgin territory. It usually faces pre-existing structures that never let go easily and continue to resist as they renew their assaults after periods of apparent dormancy. Their withdrawal is only final by the end of a series of successive slips. This is what happened in Al-Andalus. There are two moments in the evolution of the cultural project that were profiled in Cordoba: the moment of declaration with the work of Ibn Hazm, and the moment of full maturity with that of Averroes. We shall limit the present analysis to an outline of the major components of these two moments.

Ibn Hazm's dhahirism[17]: *a critical vision and a demonstrative method*

People usually consider Ibn Hazm simply as a *dhahirist* jurist and a virulent polemicist. And if some of them add a supplementary trait to the description of his intellectual personality, it is often to note the subtlety of his analysis of love and love behavior in his famous epistle *Dove's Collar.* To reduce Ibn Hazm's thought to such a level amounts to unfairly concealing—deliberately or not is of little importance—the contribution of one of the greatest innovators of Arab-Islamic thought. He could rightfully be considered as the founder of a new moment in the history of this thought. Indeed, the *dhahirism* (exotericism) of Ibn Hazm, "Cordoba's Jurist," represents, from the point of view of the political conjuncture analyzed in the preceding pages, within which his thought was based and shaped, an ideological counter-project. This ideology competed with the ideologies of both the Fatimids and the Abbassids, two historically rival states that fought over Al-Andalus and fought the Omeyyad Caliphate, mostly using ideology as a weapon. Ibn Hazm was the spokesperson of the Omeyyad state and the defender of its ideological-cultural project. From a purely epistemological point of view, one could clearly see that such *dhahirism* covered a philosophically-aimed intellectual project that hoped to reconstruct "indication" as a founding cognitive order of Sunni thought (Mu'tazilite and Ash'arite included), by providing it with a new foundation: "demonstration" (i.e., the Aristotelian syllogistic method and the scientific and philosophical conceptions that it articulates), and by radically erasing the imprint of Shi'ite and Sufi "illumination."[18]

One cannot appreciate the proper worth of Ibn Hazm's greatness unless one compares his production to that of the period's leading juridical, dogmatic, and philosophical movements throughout the entire Islamic world. Moreover, one cannot understand Ibn Hazm's innovative contribution, i.e., of his *dhahirism*—in its dichotomy of construction and deconstruction— a key moment in the history of Islamic thought, unless one considers the epistemological foundation upon which it rests. In other words, by seeing in the ideological critique formulated by Ibn Hazm but a mere circumstancial ideological critique, we would be censuring ourselves until we have examined the epistemological foundation from which it proceeds. For, in reality, and despite its polemic character, Ibn Hazm's critique of the theological and jurisprudence schools is not as much about opinions and theses as it is about the foundations and the principles from which these proceed. His *dhahirism*, therefore, is more of a critical method applied to the sources/foundations of jurisprudence than it is a literalist and conformist *dhahirism*, as imagined by those who automatically associated Ibn Hazm's *dhahirism* with that of Dawud al-'Isfahani (died 270/884). Juridically speaking, Ibn Hazm is very much tied to this school that was founded by Dawud and his son. Yet, even within this domain, the Jurist of Cordoba's *dhahirism* is distinctive in some very specific ways: it proceeds from a global vision of dogma and law, inspired by logic, by the physical sciences, and by philosophy.

To demonstrate the systematic character of Ibn Hazm's vision, it may be useful to reiterate what his positions were about the cognitive foundations upon which the "indicational"[19] vision of the Eastern thinkers lay. This vision was centered around three major principles.

the principle of discontinuity

This principle was established by the Mu'tazilite atomistic thesis (later adopted by the Ash'arites) according to which everything in the world is made up of "homogeneous" atoms that are independent from each other, between which there is only void, that possess no particular nature or quiddity, and that do not influence each other. The atoms are nothing but God-created "supports" in which God creates accidents that never last two successive instants but are perpetually recreated. This vision implies a perpetually and continually acting divine will (perpetual creation) and does not leave any room for either specific nature (*tab'*), individual nature (*tabi'a*), influence, or causality. There are only divine acts, initiated (*mubtada*) or generated (*mutawallad*), all of which proceed from divine will, including acts that are attributed to humans.

the principle of contingency

This second principle follows from the first one. Since every single thing proceeds from divine will and divine might, and since these are limitless, "reason" admits as feasible for God to mix antagonistic and contradictory things, for example for him to mix fire and cotton without a resultant combustion, a heavy rock and void without a resultant fall, or visual perception and blindness. This is what we are told by the Muʿtazilite jurist Abu al-Hudhail al-ʿAllaf,[20] then by the Ashʿarites, who made "breaking the habit" (*kharq al-ʿada*[21]) and "negation of causality" two of their fundamental principles.

the principle of analogy

The methodological principle of "indicational" thinking operates, in the cases of grammar and jurisprudence, from the principle/foundation (*asl*) to the case in point (*farʿ*), and from the known (*shahid*) to the unknown (*ghaʾib*) in the case of dialectical theology.

Ibn Hazm critiques and refutes these principles, denouncing the falsity of the results to which they lead. He rejects the atomistic thesis and its corollary, the principle of discontinuity, and proclaims along with the philosophers (with Aristotle) that substance is nothing but the body, that "every substance is body, that every body is substance and these are two names referring to the same thing"; that void has no existence: "there is no void in the world, which is a massive globe without interstices." Similarly, he refutes the theory of contingency from which is derived the negation of individual natures and of causality. Instead, he considers that "this false doctrine" is by no means justified, neither in the revealed law nor in reason, and insists that "individual natures and habits (*ʿadat*) are things that are very much created by God—His might and His grandeur be witnessed—who has arranged nature in such a way that it never alters itself (by itself), and that no reason-endowed being could conceive that it might change." As for analogy, Ibn Hazm only recognizes its validity when it operates between elements of the same species, i.e., inside a whole that includes elements of the same nature. Analogy is, however, impossible between elements from different wholes (sets) of a dissimilar nature. Hence, the falsity of analogy as it applies to jurisprudence and to dialectical theology.

The jurists establish analogies between terms of different species on the basis of their mere fortuitous affinity (*shabah*), when affinity alone is not enough to confer the same status (*hukm*) to two things. If it were the case, all things would end up receiving the same status, since there is not one thing that does not share some affinity with another. The arbitrary choice of one point of affinity between two things, which the jurists would consider as the "motive" (*'illa*) for the analogical inference, is mere conjecture. To legislate from conjecture, however, is unacceptable because the law must consist in categorical decisions that can only be based on the text itself. As for the theologians' analogical reasoning (*qiyas*), it is no less futile because the nature of the known (the world of man) being *other* than that of the unknown (the divine world) , there can be no analogy between them. These two worlds are at opposite ends of each other: man's world which is imperfect and corruptible versus God's world which is pure perfection and everlasting.

It is clear that what Ibn Hazm aims at, beyond his critique of the cognitive principles, are the jurisprudence schools and the theological trends that were based upon their principles and which partook of the Abbassid cultural and ideological enterprise (the Hanafite and Shafi'ite schools, the Mu'tazilites and the Ash'arites' dialectical theology). Ibn Hazm displays an asperity that verges on virulence in his critique of these schools and these trends, judging—as any reader would note—by the treatise which he devoted to the science of the sources/foundations, *Al-Ihkam fi usul al-ahkam;* by his law encyclopedia, *Al-Muhalla*; and by his polemic theological work, *Al-Fisal fi al-milal wa al-ahwa' wa al-nihal.* But there is no need to linger over this point. Let us just focus on that part of this critique that can be considered as an invitation to "uprising" and "revolt" against the "official" schools of jurisprudence, and hence against the authority of the state (the Abbassid state), which drew its religious legitimacy from its membership in this or that school. Let us discuss the highly virulent critique that Ibn Hazm launches against "imitation" (*taqlid*) as used by these schools. "No man is allowed," Ibn Hazm asserts, "to imitate someone else, living or dead, but each must perform, to the best of his ability, an interpretative effort (*ijtihad*)." He who does not possess the science of the jurists must ask these about what the law says. The jurists owe him an explanation of the best way to derive a judgment from the text, in order that he may properly appreciate its accuracy and personally arrive at a decision related to his question. Thus he would have assumed his responsibility and exercised his interpretative effort to the best of his means. "Those," he adds, "who claim that it is consistent with religion for a common man to imitate a jurisconsult (*mufti*) are totally wrong and are not sanctioned by either Qur'anic texts, data from the hadith, or consensus (*ijma*). Their point of view cannot even be justified by analogical reasoning. Under these conditions, they are wrong because they make a judgment without proof." The author then adds: "Let anyone who imitates a companion, a follower, a Malik, an Abu Hanifa, a Shafi'i, a Sufyan,[22] an Awza'i, an Ahmad (Ibn Hanbal), or a Dawud (al-Isfahani)—may God be satisfied with them—know that all of the above people 'wash their hands' of him, in this world as well as in the other world."

What remains to be mentioned is Ibn Hazm's critique of the epistemological foundation of the Fatimid Caliphate's ideology and of the illuminationist thought in general. Ibn Hazm loudly and clearly proclaims that:

> God's (praise be to Him) religion is purely exoteric and is by no means esoteric. It is entirely obvious and hides no latent secret. It is entirely based on proof and nothing in it is left to chance. God's Messenger (God's prayers and peace be upon Him) did not conceal any meaning of the revealed law, subtle though it may have been. There is not anything either which he may have shared with his closest relatives, wife, daughter, uncle or cousin, that he did not share with the average people, white or black, or

with a mere shepherd. There is no secret, no hidden meaning that the Prophet—peace be upon him—may have opted not to divulge. All his message was delivered in the preaching that he addressed to all, because if he had concealed anything, we might as well say that he had not fulfilled his mission.

Ibn Hazm thus dismantles the pairing of the concepts of manifest/latent (*dhahir/batin*) upon which the illuminationist thought of the Shi'ites and the Sufis was based. As for the "inspiration" (*ilham*) that is generally claimed by the illuminationists, it is totally without foundation and untenable. We cannot consider it as a source of knowledge to be imposed on all, since any and everybody could very well claim to have received an inspiration that negates the inspiration of someone else, without the latter being able to prove the veracity of his inspiration other than by what he asserts. Thus, the principle of the imam's "instructor function" (*ta'lim*)[23] loses its foundation altogether, since nothing proves the veracity of the imam's sayings other than the fact that they were inspired to him. But inspiration is without foundation, as we have seen.

Ibn Hazm, therefore, refutes all the cognitive principles upon which the Imamist and Battinist Shi'ites base their thinking, the same way he refutes the founding principles of the "Sunni" dogma that was adopted by the Abbassid state. But what does he propose as a "carry-on" alternative?

All of Ibn Hazm's thought—and not only his juridical doctrine—is based upon the following cognitive principle—

There are only two ways to have access to sure knowledge: (1) the primary data of reason and the senses; and (2) the premises that follow from these.

The primary data of reason and the senses enable us to distinguish the properties of every living thing, and we must refer to it to find out "the reality of the properties of things and to decide, should the situation arise, on the impossibility of a thing." Ibn Hazm applies this principle to the knowledge of nature as well as to the confirmation of the dogma and to the understanding of the law (*shari'a*).

Whether our knowledge of natural phenomena depends on the primary data of reason and the senses or on the premises that follow from these, it is an obvious truth granted by the sciences of nature which Ibn Hazm has no problem admitting and in fact finds useful, even indispensable to human existence, since they are based on observation, experience and demonstration. Ibn Hazm further explains that our knowledge of the dogma proceeds also from the primary data of reason and the senses and from the resulting premises. It is true that "through the perception of tangible and intelligible things and through the knowledge of features that are usually attributed to them," we are able to establish "the creation of the world, the oneness and the eternity of the Creator, the reality of the prophethood of He whose prophethood was confirmed by proof," all being principles of the dogma. As for the law, we must distinguish between what is apprehensible by reason and what is not. Reason is not enough to account for "the licit or illicit character of pork (...) or for the fact that the midday prayer calls for four genuflections (*rak'a*s) while the sunset prayer only calls for three (...); none of this falls within the scope of reason. It is not up to reason to understand why such a thing was imposed or forbidden." In the same way, in the natural world, it is not within its scope "that man has to have two eyes rather than three." This "does not fall within the scope of reason either, and it is not up to it to understand why things are this way and not otherwise." But this does not mean that reason has no role whatsoever to play in legal matters. The law functions following the same rules as nature. The same way we can, by observing natural phenomena, infer general rules that are applicable to all similar phenomena that we have not observed, the same way there are prescriptions within the law that are explicitly imposed by the text, which we must consider as legal data that should not be modified or changed either through analogical reasoning (*qiyas*), through consensus (*ijma'*), or through some other operation. There are also those cases which are not explicitly accounted for in the law and the solutions of which depend on "proof" (*dalil*) to be sought inside the legislative texts from which a first premise will be drawn. The second premise is to be drawn either from the text again, or from the primary data of reason.

Ibn Hazm thus creates four combinations of premises, the premises of syllogism in jurisprudence, assumable in the demonstrative procedure (*dalil*):

(1) the two premises are drawn from the legislative text;
(2) one of the premises is drawn from the legislative text and the other from the primary data of reason;
(3) one of the premises is about a consensus and the other is an injunction, formulated by the legislative text, to follow the consensus; and
(4) one of the premises is a general designation and the other is a specific case under the jurisdiction of such designation. It is from these pairs of premises that one constructs the demonstrative syllogism.

"Proof," or "demonstration," as applied to the juridical practice by the Cordoban jurist, is thus established. He confirms that "there is no access to a sure knowledge, in matters of religious prescriptions (*ahkam*), outside of these four combinations (of premises). They are all linked to the text, which we know to be a mandatory reference, and whose meaning is apprehensible by reason following the procedure that we have shown." Ibn Hazm therefore acknowledges three sources/foundations for legislation: the Book, the hadith and "proof." We already know that he did not acknowledge the validity of analogy (*qiyas*). But for consensus (*ijma'*), Ibn Hazm constructs a specific conception: he does not mean the jurists' consensus at a given time, which would be unreachable and impossible, but either the consensus among Muslims about certain cultural practices explicitly prescribed by the text, such as prayer or fasting, etc., or the consensus among the companions on a prophetic saying or action which they witnessed, or which was reported according to them by way of someone who did not know the Prophet personally. "These are the two kinds of consensus and no others can exist."

"Proof" is thus "drawn from the text or from consensus" and there is no room for personal opinion (*ra'y*) or for analogy (*qiyas*)." Even consensus itself "cannot be established except upon the faith of a text," which confirms the fact that the companions were in unanimous agreement about a given point. Therefore, there are no religious prescriptions whatsoever that do not directly proceed from the text.

Is this rigorism or intransigence? Not in the slightest. By confining himself so closely to the text, Ibn Hazm considerably widens the field of the "permissible" (*mubah*). He considers that every single thing was originally permissible and that it is not within the jurisdiction of reason to find it licit or illicit. Then came religion, which decreed the licitness or illicitness of certain things. Anything that escapes these rules, however, remains permissible. Then Ibn Hazm adds that "this is a truth that is naturally recognized by reason; and so it dispenses with confirmation from analogy or opinion."

Whether we approve of Ibn Hazm or not, we must in any case recognize him as the pioneer of a new era of critique within the Arab-Islamic culture: a global critique of the vision and the methodology of "illumination" in its double form, Shi'ite and Sufi; and a no-less global critique of the themes and methods of dialectical theology, of juridical analogy, and of imitation. Ibn Hazm's aim was not to critique for the sake of critiquing, but rather to overcome the growth crises of the Arab-Islamic culture and to propose a method of reconstruction that consists in basing "indication" on "demonstration" in order to eradicate "illumination" once and for all. To this end, Ibn Hazm prescribed the method of syllogism and inductive examination, in addressing both dogma and jurisprudence. Moreover, he encouraged the adoption of the existing sciences (Aristotle's physical sciences) to construct a new, well-informed, "indicational" vision that agreed with the principles of religion the way they are literally enunciated, allowed dogmatic openness, and did not impede human action. Such freedom was enjoyed within the field of the "permissible," a field that was to expand indefinitely with the evolution of knowledge and society's development.

It is therefore not a question, as may be believed, of a literalist and intransigent *dhahirism* (exotericism) that would restrain the field of reason, but in fact a rational critical attitude, tied to the text, and only to the text, when the text addresses a given item, i.e., in the end, and in Ibn Hazm's own words, in very few cases. What is left from the hold of the text is limitless, pertains to man's freedom, and is left to reason and to free choice.

It is this rational critical attitude that chooses to base "indicational" vision and method upon "demonstration" that Averroes would later attempt to develop and draw from it the necessary conclusions.

The Averroist rationalism and the re-arrangement of the relationship of religion-philosophy

Ibn Hazm's *dhahirism* could not have achieved the spread and the intellectual appropriation that it claimed at a time when the Omeyyad Empire, for which Ibn Hazm was the spokesman representing its ideological project, was in its final days. Such a global and systematic ideological project that claimed to have imposed itself on all of the social body could not have been realized without the support of a political regime. Ibn Hazm knew well that the jurisprudence schools, which managed to acquire legal power within a given society, had only spread thanks to the authority of the state. "Two schools," he said "flourished, thanks to the regime, Malik's school in the West and Abu Hanifa's in the East." He understood that the regime likely to impose his doctrine had reached the end of its existence and could not be resuscitated. This led him to bitterness and despair. He said, speaking of himself: "As for my situation, one cannot describe it better than by quoting the famous proverb: the first ones to dislike a scholar are his own. I have read in the Bible that Jesus—may peace be upon him— said 'a prophet is nowhere despised but in his own house, in his own land'; the hardships endured by the prophet (sl'm) from the Quraysh [tribe] confirm this certainty."

But great intellectual projects that are critical and innovative do not die with their conceivers. They only need "some time" for that historical moment favorable for their flourishing to come. Ibn Hazm's *dhahirism* was one such project. That is why it is not surprising to see that, a little more than half a century later, it inspired the political and revolutionary movement led by the "Mahdi" Ibn Tumart in Morocco in the year 511/1117. This movement was launched against the regime of the Almoravid monarchs. The Andalusian nobles, scholars, jurists and politicians had appealed to the Almoravids to put an end to the "fratricide" wars that divided the land during the time of the kings of Taifas, immediately after the fall of the Omeyyad Caliphate. Although the administrative and political apparatus of the Almoravid dynasty (of Saharan origin) may have been heavily subjected to the purview of the Malikite jurists who were only slightly "rigorist," from the doctrinal standpoint "civilization, luxury and indolence"—according to Ibn Khaldun—soon sneaked into their courts and from then on into the whole of society, which became "contaminated with the epidemics of carelessness." Ibn Tumart rose against this situation and accused the Almoravids of having deviated from true religion, basing his political action on the principle of "the commandment of good and the interdiction of evil."[24] He also accused them of "imitative conformism" (*taqlid*) and of "anthropomorphism" (*tajsim*), denouncing the fact that the doctrine behind their regime had been based on analogy. The Almoravids had established the opinions of their Malikite jurists as sources of analogy and, by so doing, had leaned towards "imitation," abandoning the true sources: the Qur'an and the hadith. They had furthermore based their dogma on analogy of the known to the unknown, which amounts to positing divine attributes as analogous to human attributes, a fact that, according to Ibn Tuumart, was sheer anthropomorphism.

Starting from this principle, which was directly inspired by the epistemological core of Ibn Hazm's *dhahirism*, Ibn Tuumart led his movement to fruition, i.e., the founding of the Almohad state which, for the sake of its own intellectual strategy, took over Ibn Hazm's project. The *dhahirist* doctrine thus finally found the political support that it needed to impose itself, i.e., the Almohad state. The Almohads, shortly after settling in Morocco and in Al-Andalus, became high-handed with the Malikite school and restricted the spread of jurisprudence books in order to push the population, in legal practice, to stick to the sources: the Qur'an and the hadith. This new cultural policy reached its highest point at the time of Ya'qub al-Mansur, the third Almohad caliph, under whose reign jurisprudence totally ceased to exist. This ruler, who was dreaded by jurists, ordered the burning of the Malikite-school books and called upon all scholars to renounce any practice of the "science of personal opinion" (*analogy*), or else be severely punished. Ya'qub's goal was in fact to abolish, to remove once and for all, the Malikite doctrine from the Maghreb (and from Al-Andalus), in order to force the population to follow the manifest (*dhahir*) meaning of the Qur'an and the hadith.

But the cultural policy led by the Almohads was not limited to combating the practice of "jurisprudence" and "imitation" in favor of a return to the sources, i.e., to the "manifest meaning of the Qur'an and the hadith." The Almohads became equally open to the "sciences of the ancient ones," gave freer rein to philosophy and, during the reigns of Abu Ya'qub Yusuf Ibn 'Abd al-Mu'min and his son Ya'qub al-Mansur, began to collect large quantities of books on philosophy and the ancient sciences. They soon owned as large a collection as that of the (above mentioned) Omeyyad Caliph al-Hakam al-Mustansir. The Almohad Caliph did not collect books for decorative purposes. He read them; as a matter of fact, he was an impassioned adept of philosophy. Having noticed "the confusion of the Aristotelian discourse" and Aristotle's "abstruse subjects," he commissioned Cordoba's philosopher, Abu al-Walid Ibn Rushd, Averroes, to paraphrase this author. It was the return to the "sources" of philosophy and the renunciation of the "imitation" of Eastern philosophers.

It is worth noting at this point that the rulers of the Maghreb, from the beginning of the Almoravid dynasty—founded by Yusuf Ibn Tashfin who annexed Al-Andalus to his empire—customarily sent their eldest sons as seconds-in-command in Al-Andalus. The future caliphs were thus educated in this land among scholars and philosophers. There is therefore a direct and organic link between the intellectual school that had been established in Cordoba from the time of the Omeyyads, and the cultural policy adopted by the Almohads: the enlightened Almohad caliphs had been educated in Cordoba, under the guidance of its scholars and philosophers. It was these learned men who made up the caliph's learned court. Let us add that the same factors that had already contributed in a significant way to the creation of the Andalusian cultural project at the time of the Omeyyads would intervene again to guide the cultural policy of the Almohads: the conflict and the competition that existed between the Almohad caliphate and its Fatimid and Abbassid homologues remained perennial ones. This antagonism was to continue as one of the constants of the politics of the states in Al-Andalus and in the Maghreb.

After this historical reminder, which is necessary to shed light on the element of continuity between the Hazmian and the Averroist developments, we shall describe the major elements of the Averroist project, focusing on the epistemological significance of the latter, the same way we did already for that of Ibn Hazm.

Let us note from the beginning that the Averroist discourse, even if it follows Ibn Hazm's project in approach and in orientation, by far surpasses the latter in method and in content. This is not only due to the evolution of theoretical thinking in Al-Andalus during the period that separates the two men; it also reflects the transformations that had occurred within Eastern thinking during that same period. Averroes encounters a situation that did not exist during Ibn Hazm's time. He must face the Avicennian "conciliationism" and its gnostic residues and counter Ghazali's offensive against philosophy and philosophers. All this had to be added to the task with which he was officially and publicly entrusted: "to remove confusion from Aristotle's discourse."

Averroes' work could be divided into four major areas:

(1) to comment on Aristotle's work and "facilitate its comprehension by common folks";
(2) to show that Avicenna did "deviate" from the foundations of philosophy and that he did not follow the demonstrative method;
(3) to refute Ghazali by proving the "incoherence"[25] of his objections to philosophers and by showing that the Ash'arite method represented a deviation from the path that the revelation showed to common folks, and remained incapable of reaching with any measure of certainty; and
(4) to design a new method that consisted of revealing the processes of demonstration (used by the Qur'an) so as to present the dogma of religion,[26] a method based upon two principles: "to observe the apparent meaning" of the text while taking into consideration "the intention of the legislator." Thus he re-arranged the relationship between wisdom (philosophy) and religion, following the principle according to which each of them proceeds from its own principles and uses its own method of reasoning, even if both aim at the same thing: to inspire virtue.

Let us now "fly" over each of those "continents" explored by Averroes's thought:

1. The major characteristic of Averroes's thought is unquestionably his systematic outlook on things and his axiomatic method, both being expressions of a concern to consider given parts through the whole to which they belonged. There is no doubt that this intellectual approach, mathematically-minded, was the result of the efforts of those Andalusians scholars who, as we pointed out earlier, approached the ancient sciences through mathematics and logic, far from the polemics of theologians and from the problematics of conciliating reason and transmission. "It is advisable," Averroes writes, "that all those who have chosen to search for the truth (...) when they find themselves facing statements that seem inadmissible to them, avoid the systematic rejection of such statements and try to understand them through the path which, according to their authors, leads to the search for truth. In order to reach conclusive results, they must devote all the time necessary and follow the order required by the studied question." It is by following this methodical process that the philosopher will be able to understand religious questions from within the religious discourse and that the religious man will be able to comprehend the philosophical theses from within the system where they fit.

We will thus have a better understanding of what our philosopher calls the "demonstrative method," which he never fails to praise every time he critiques the Eastern thinkers' methods. We are not talking about an ordinary deductive reasoning, but a hypothetical deductive method that is well-defined and consciously applied, which we would call the axiomatic method today. According to Averroes, any other method is nothing but "dialectics" or "rhetoric." The reasoning use by Avicenna and the theologians is nothing else but the dialectical method of the Greek sophists. This axiomatic vision extends to all the topics that Averroes treated in his writings. Is it not telling that he wrote only the *Colliget* (*Kulliyat*) of medicine, i.e., its general principles, leaving the writing of the applications and the specific cases to Ibn Zuhr, his contemporary? Averroes preferred to confine himself to theoretical medicine because it suited better his concern for axiomatization. And what is more, it is medicine itself that is axiomatically defined by him. Medicine to him "is a (professional) practice that must be based on true principles," and not only on experience and on trial and error. "His aim is not to necessarily (and directly) heal, but to do what is necessary within the necessary proportions, when it is necessary, then wait for the results, as is the case in the science of navigation or the science of military command." Indeed, the human body upon which it is practiced is not a simple body, it is a system. If the equilibrium of this system is disrupted by disease, medicine intervenes, not to re-establish this equilibrium through its own action but to help the body re-establish, by itself, the equilibrium that is inherent in it.

The axiomatic approach is similarly apparent in Averroes's law treatise entitled: *Bidayat al-mujtahid wa nihayat al-muqtasid* (Beginning of the striver [for a personal judgment], end of the contented [with the received teaching]), in which the author presents the viewpoints of the different schools of jurisprudence while defending them within the system to which they belong. It is a unique book on the subject and an enormous piece of work carried out by the synthetic spirit of a man of genius.

It is also through this method that Averroes comments on the works of Aristotle, not as a collection of themes that are separated from each other, but as a coherent system. He read Aristotle through Aristotle, i.e., by referring to the foundations of his philosophy, to all of his opinions and by comparing these to each other. He also compared the various Arabic translations to each other, a fact that enabled him to rid the *Magister Primus'* philosophy from the alterations and the interpretations that previous commentators, like Avicenna, had inflicted on it. Any careful reader of Averroes's commentaries would readily understand that the admiration for Aristotle by this philosopher was less motivated by the fact that he approved of this or that opinion of the Master's than by his willingness to show that all of his opinions were clearly part and parcel of one system that is endowed with internal coherence. What drew Averroes toward Aristotle was his demonstrative method, which he believed to be the only one capable of guaranteeing the acquisition of science and certainty.

Having said that, we should also point out the fact that Averroes was not a mere commentator or a mere disciple of the Master. If he defends Aristotle's theses, it is very often to prove that they are legitimate within their system, and not to declare that they are true in the absolute. The methodical principle that guides him in all his commentaries and his refutations is the following statement which he attributes to the Master himself, in *The Incoherence of the Incoherence:* "To be fair consists in seeking arguments in favor of the opponent as one would for oneself." Indeed, Averroes considered Aristotle as an "opponent" as well as a "friend." A friend, because he saw in him a great philosopher whose only goal was the search for truth; as such, Aristotle was a *mujtahid,* a researcher who practices *ijtihad* (interpretive effort) over the "book of the universe." An opponent, because Averroes was well aware that not all the principles upon which Aristotle based his search for the truth were compatible with Islam. Aristotle and Averroes are friends in so far as they both follow the same path and aim at the same thing: the truth. But what makes them different is that each path proceeds from its own principles and each has its own system of reference. And this is precisely the kind of relationship that Averroes establishes between philosophy and religion. This ambivalent feeling toward Aristotle is reflected when reading Averroes: he is concerned about respecting the *Magister Primus'* system, so he finds himself compelled to interpret, without distorting them, those of Aristotle's theses which do not concur with Muslim dogma. The interpretation of Aristotle's discourse now takes on a new dimension, that of reducing to the minimum the differences between the viewpoints of religion and Aristotle. Yet at times the task proves to be impossible. Averroes then hopes to excuse Aristotle by proving that the axioms which he (Aristotle) had posited as principles, inevitably implied that he had arrived at such conclusions. As Averroes often insists, these are not true in the absolute. Their veracity is conditioned by the system from which they are derived.

Averroes's main concern, therefore, was not to defend Aristotle at all costs, but to understand him. It is through his efforts at understanding and interpretation that this philosopher's originality is best manifested. There were many ideas conceived by Averroes himself that he attributed to Aristotle, simply so that these could become a part of the Aristotelian system and be able to bridge the gap between the said-system and the Muslim vision. In sum, there is a profoundly and specifically Averroist philosophy in his commentaries of Aristotle, a philosophy that is fundamentally rationalist, Muslim and Maghrebian by its problematics.

2. Now we understand in the name of which principle Averroes critiques Avicenna, the "great master." According to the Cordoban philosopher, the "great master" had not followed the demonstrative method when presenting the philosophers' opinions. He had limited himself to the theologians' method, i.e., the two-term analogical reasoning, a process which amounts to equating two totally heterogeneous worlds, the visible and the invisible. Whereas analogy, according to Averroes, is only valid "when the passage from one term to the other is obvious, i.e., when the nature of the 'known' is identical to that of the 'unknown.'" Averroes rejects, in the name of this methodological critique, all the concepts that Avicenna implemented to reconcile religious and philosophical notions. These concepts were based on the postulate of the existence of a third value that causes

two contradictory notions to agree, a fact that led Avicenna to think of notions such as: "created in itself eternal in time," "the possible by itself necessary by others," "knowledge of specific things in a universal way," and "the possibility of proceeding from the multiple to the One by emanation." Let us indeed dwell a little on Averroes's critique of the epistemological foundations of Avicenna's notional apparatus, so that we can realize that through such critique the rupture that is created then leads to a point of no return.

To prove that the world is created by God, theologians had wanted to prove that it had a beginning. But to say that the world, as an act of God, had a beginning raised serious difficulties. Why had God created the world at a given moment and not at another? Besides, to say that a someone did something "before" or "after" implies that such act had a motive. God, however, in his very essence, is exempt from "motivation."

In order to overcome these difficulties, Avicenna had proposed the concept of the "created in itself eternal in time." According to him, "the world considered as such is created, (but) considered in relation to time, is eternal." For Averroes, this an is illusory problem that proceeds from erroneous reasoning. Indeed, he thinks that Avicenna and the theologians equated the beginning of the world as a whole with the beginning of things of this world. By "beginning," they meant the fact of "being created in time and from nothing." Used this way, the term indeed applies to the worldly things but not the world as a whole. In fact, to say that things begin is to say that they change and become transformed. However, to say that the world has a beginning is to say that it is an act of God, an act without any relationship to time. "For He whose being does not take place in time and is not circumscribed by it, his act must, of necessity, be not circumscribed by time and must not take place in a well-defined time." It is therefore in order to distinguish between the beginning of the world and that of worldly things that the (ancient) philosophers preferred to say that the world is eternal.

To avoid this confusion and to overcome the afore-mentioned difficulties, Averroes proposes to posit that the world as a whole is "in perpetual beginning," knowing very well that the theologians would not have accepted this thesis. They could not indeed conceive of a change without beginning or end, "a perpetual creation," because they used to equate the metaphysical world with the physical one, or creation in the sense of "act of God" with creation in the sense of "appearance and re-appearance" of things in the world. This is why "if we were to check carefully the theologians' thesis, we would learn that they conceive of God as an eternal human being. Indeed, they equate the world with things made by man, by his will, his science and his power. When they are told that our God (thus conceived) should be a body, they reply that He is eternal whereas everybody is created. They must therefore assume the existence of a man without body, an agent of everything that is, and this is nothing but a metaphor and a poetic expression."

The "perpetual beginning" proposed by Averroes to resolve the problem of creation does raise the question of the infinite, and our philosopher is well aware of it. But, according to him, this question is only asked of those who think of the metaphysical world by reference to data from the physical world. Of course, "it is impossible, for us humans, to conceive of the infinite as an act since our respective kinds and levels of knowledge are separate from one another. But if we assume a science in which all levels and kinds of knowledge are gathered, the finite and the infinite are but one with regard to this "science.""

Averroes re-addresses the question, so often raised by the theologians, from a more mathematical perspective. Theologians claimed that the atom must be indivisible, otherwise the infinite (the atoms of one body) would be greater than the infinite (the atoms of a smaller body), which is impossible. Once again, this is false reasoning whose "falsity obtains because the theologians mistake the continuous for the discontinuous and believe that what is necessary for one is necessary for the other. But the notions of 'more numerous' or 'less numerous' are only valid for discontinuous quantities, that is for numbers; as for continuous quantities, one ought to say that they are 'greater' or 'smaller,' but not 'more numerous' or 'less numerous.'" The body, which is a continuous quantity, could not possibly be more or less numerous than another body. It may be equal, greater or smaller. Without this distinction between the continuous and the discontinuous, "things would all be numbers; there would be absolutely no continuous quantities, and geometry would be reduced to arithmetic."

Avicenna was pleased to have succeeded in proving, through a "simple logical division," the existence of God and the creation of the world, while avoiding the complications involved in this process. This division consisted in distinguishing three kinds of being: the being [that is] necessary by itself (God), the being [that is] possible by itself (worldly things) and the being [that is] possible by itself and necessary by others (the world). Avicenna would thus say that "the world being possible by itself, is created; but being necessary by others (by God) is eternal." He was then talking about a third value introduced between the notions of necessity and possibility of which both Aristotle and Farabi had spoken.

For Averroes, "This adjunction is superfluous and erroneous because, no matter how we consider it, the necessary cannot possess any features of possibility. There is not one thing which is endowed with a unique nature, of whose nature one could say that it is both possible and necessary (...) for the possible is the opposite of the necessary." Moreover, the possible is not likely to be necessary, by itself or by others, unless its nature were to become that of the necessary, something that is impossible. Similarly, the necessary cannot become possible "for there is absolutely no possible in the necessary natures, be they necessary through itself or through others."

The Muslim thinkers from the East had abundantly discussed the question of causality. For the Mu'tazilites, the rationalists of Islam, man is free; he creates his acts and he is responsible for them. But acts result from a chain of causes and effects: consequently, what happens to the original act that started this chain? And would the agent of such act be responsible for all the "generated acts"? The issue of the "generating of acts" (*tawlid*) thus began and became the earliest formulation of the problem of causality in Islam.

As for the Ash'arite theologians, they defended a disguised fatalism. While their ambiguous doctrine on the one hand stated that God is the only agent and that man does not create his acts (no one can do what God enabled him to do), on the other hand they insisted that man must assume responsibility for all acts that are assigned unto him. This is what they called "acquisition" (*kasb*). To the notion of "acquisition," which amounts to actually denying man's freedom, corresponds the notion of "habit" (*'ada*), at the level of physical phenomena. The "generated acts" are not due to the relationship of cause and effect, but are created by God. This way, the miraculous act (*mu'jiza*) of prophets remained possible; it was a non-habitual act, a sign that proved prophecy.

In order to prove the possibility of the "miracle" (*mu'jiza*), Ghazali, the major authority of Ash'arite theology, had rejected the philosophical thesis of the necessary relationship from cause to effect. He explains this as follows: We are in the habit of saying that fire burns cotton, but nothing leads us to believe with certainty that fire is indeed the cause of combustion. All that we can state is that cotton burns when it is touched by fire, but this does not imply that cotton burns because of fire: "it burns in fire and not by fire." Consequently, it is very likely that cotton will not burn—if God wills it—even if it is thrown into fire. Such a phenomenon which is possible by itself, willed by God and unusual to us, is called a miracle. It is a gift which the prophets possess to convince humans of their prophethood.

Averroes, as an intransigent rationalist, rises above such discourse and replies that negation of causality is not a way to prove prophecy.

Indeed, a miracle is not the proof but the sign of prophecy. We must therefore believe in it *a priori* and then ask whoever claims to be a prophet to show us the extraordinary sign of his prophethood. The miracle that Muhammad performed is, in the opinion of all Muslims, the Qur'an, which has no relationship to causality. In short, if one does not *a priori* believe in prophecy, all miraculous acts remain merely part of a magic realm. Besides, those who reject causality forget that without it the existence of God is impossible to prove, for, without causality, one cannot establish the existence of secondary causes which follow from the primary cause. Without causality, the world is pure contingency and chance and the very notion of a creator remains conjectural, superfluous and void of meaning.

But let us skip the details of this polemics and let us examine carefully Averroes's ideas on this philosophical and scientific question. He defends causality from two perspectives: epistemology and ontology.

From an epistemological point of view, science, to him, is not possible unless one recognizes the principle of causality; for "knowledge of the effects could not be perfect without the knowledge of the causes. To deny this (causality) is to declare science vain and to suspend it." Definition, demonstration, and the distinction between things, their properties; all of this is based on the principle of causality. Averroes wonders hence about the notion of habit ('ada): "I wonder what they (theologians) mean by the term 'habit.'" Is it the Agent's [God] habit? But his is not conceivable for God, because habit is a faculty that is acquired by repetition and God is exempt from such behavior. Is it the habit of things? This is not possible, for one speaks of habit only in reference to living things. Speaking of inanimates, one says that they have a nature. But theologians unanimously reject the view of the "naturalists" who claim that everything that exists owes its existence to its own nature. If in the end we mean by this the habit—that is inherent to ourselves—of judging things, "habit therefore would be nothing but that act of intelligence, implied by the very nature of the latter, by which intelligence is intelligence." Understood as such, intelligence is nothing less than the principle of causality. Consequently, to speak of it no longer makes sense, for "to substitute one word for another makes no difference whatsoever as long as the content remains the same."

Yet, if we were to transfer "habit"—as discussed—from the epistemological to the ontological level, this would entail, according to Averroes, negating the objective existence of things, "because the existence of things is based only on the fact that they are in (causal) relationship to one another." That is why he insists on the necessity of believing in causality at the ontological level; for to say that things owe their causal relationship to that "psychological habit" alone would have the disastrous outcome of claiming that "the living are merely conventional."

In line with his conception of an ontological causality, Averroes compares the world to a cobweb woven by causality. The essence of the world is therefore pure harmony. And it is by discovering this order, prevalent in the world, that man shapes his knowledge. We must however realize that our soul often believes that such opinions are indeed necessary judgments, and this is because of our ignorance.

"Therefore, if by 'habit' the Ash'arite theologians meant this kind of unnecessary judgments, but which our soul believes necessary, we would accept their opinion of causality. But if by this they want to reject the very possibility of any necessary judgment, we shall tell them: You, who make the statement that nothing is necessary, must consider your own statement as unnecessary," Averroes concludes.

In this case, does causality not question man's freedom once again? To answer this question we must clarify what is meant by "free choice." For Averroes, as well as for all Muslim thinkers, to be free means to be able to fulfill one's will. But "man's will," he writes, "is but a desire that is stimulated unto him from the outside, including from his own body." And "This desire is satisfied whenever causal relationships, within and outside of his body, allow it."

Is freedom therefore a prisoner of chance? No, because in Averroes's thinking, there is no room for fortuitous events. Everything is linked by cause-and-effect relationships. Freedom itself is included in this causal network which gives it meaning and makes it intelligible. As a reasonable being, man is endowed with a faculty that enables him to progressively discover when and how causal relationships agree with his desire. This faculty is none other than reason which is itself nothing more than the knowledge of causes. Each time man knows the real causes, he becomes able to satisfy his desires, to fulfill his will; and this is what his freedom consists of.

To say that the world is created by God raised a thorny problem: that of the one and the multiple, i.e., how can we conceive that a multiple and ever-changing world can be derived from a simple, change-exempt act (that of God)?

To resolve this problem, the Muslim philosophers from the East borrowed the idea of emanation *(fayd)* from Plotinus and made of it a theory upon which the whole philosophy of being and of knowledge was based. According to this theory, the necessary being, the First Principle, endowed with an existence that is absolutely complete and with virtues that are absolutely perfect, could not—given his wisdom and his generosity—contain all these virtues within his essence. "He had to necessarily spread them all over, like clarity and light that necessarily emanate from the sun." Thus, "From the First (God), the first Intellect emanates and being conscious of its principle, causes the emanation of another Intellect (the second one), which, being conscious of itself, generates a celestial sphere, soul and body." This process continues up to the tenth Intellect, the "shape-maker," to the raw material *(hylè)*. For Avicenna, emanation is tripartite. Each emanating intellect, "becoming conscious of its principle, gives birth to another intellect, then conscious of itself as being necessary by its principle, gives birth to a soul; and conscious of itself as being possible in itself, generates a celestial body," and so on up to the tenth Intellect, the "shape-maker."

Averroes refuses to even discuss the emanation theory, which he labels as "fables and assertions that are even more inconsistent than the theologian discourse." For him, the problem of the one and the multiple had already been raised by the ancient philosophers in response to certain adepts of dualistic conceptions (e.g., the dualism between good and evil), who objected that the multiple could not possibly originate in the one. And if the philosophers of the Muslim East had once again encountered this problematic, it was not related to the context within which the ancient ones had created it, but was because they were proceeding from an analogical reasoning that consisted in equating the metaphysical with the physical. "And so," Averroes goes on to say, "Farabi and Avicenna, who had espoused their opponents' (the theologians) view according to which the agent within the domain of the 'unknown' (the metaphysical) proceeds in the same way as the agent within the domain of the 'known' (the physical) and according to which only one act originates in only one agent, could not see how the multiple could originate in the first, who is in everyone's opinion one and simple." Nothing is more wrong than this view, "for there is no common ground between the agent who, in the physical world, performs only one action and the primary agent. The latter is absolutely free, the former is not, since his acts are always predetermined. Hence, only one absolute act may originate in the absolute agent, His power of action must not be seen as being limited to such or such type of action"; for we are actually dealing with "a spiritual force that innervates the whole universe."

Averroes further explains: "Things that cannot exist without being linked to one another, like form and matter and all worldly things, depend for existence on the bond that unites them. If that is the case, he who gives the bond by the same token gives existence. It is therefore necessary that there be only one being whose existence depends on nothing. It is equally necessary that this being dispense only one gift (act or force) whose unity varies according to each being and his own nature; and that from this unique gift—dispensed unto each one— all beings draw their existence. They spread over all the way to the Primary Unity (God)."

Did Averroes believe in the "universal soul"? We do not think so. He compares the universe to a well-organized city, and God to the city-chief. God's will is spread throughout the universe just as would be the orders of the city-chief throughout society. We are therefore dealing with a spiritual force that is diffused throughout the whole universe, connecting the parts to one another while maintaining their existence. "There has to be," he says, "a spiritual force that inner-vates the parts of the world, just as there exists a force within the animal that unites its parts. The difference between the two forces lies with the fact that the link of the universe is eternal because the one who maintains it is eternal."

To know all events, all things, the slightest breath, the smallest idea or action, is to be all-knowing. God alone is all-knowing. But the world is in perpetual change, and to know the world assumes that the knowledge of he who knows is exposed to these changes. But God, by his very essence, is exempt from change altogether. Now then, how can we imagine that He is all-knowing while his knowl-edge has to be absolutely immutable?

This question was the last of the theologians' concerns, and their discourse was to insist that God knows all, things as well as events, actions as well as intentions, that nothing can escape his science, all to justify the dogma of the final judgment. To the philosophers, how-ever, to say that God knows the particular beings, with all the changes they undergo, implies that God's science would change and that as a result, his essence would be subject to change, something that is incompatible with the idea of God. Farabi clearly asserts this, as fol-lows: the object of God's science is that principles are what governs changes, but that things do not change. In order to reconcile these two contradictory theses, Farabi's and the theologians,' Avicenna, the "great master," had proposed the following solution: "God knows everything, from the smallest atom to the greatest body (the particular), and this [he knows] in a universal manner."

Such verbal reconciling could not possibly be accepted by a logician who is so concerned with rigor. For Averroes, it is once again an illusory problem resulting from the type of reasoning that consists in equating divine science with human science, despite their difference in nature. "Our science," he writes, "is (an effect) caused by the known thing. Its creation is thus subordinated to that of the thing and it changes as the thing changes. But the science that God—may He be glorified—has of the universe is the reverse of that. It is (by itself) what causes the known thing, which is also the existing thing. He who equates one of these sciences with the other is like he who equates the essences of two opposites, and this is the height of ignorance.

In the eyes of Averroes. the mistake made by the theologians, by Farabi and by Avicenna, is due to their use of nonrigorously defined terminology. For them, "to know" is to perceive things in their juxtaposition, whereas it should be: to clearly discern the order and harmony that prevail within and among them. True knowledge aims at the link between things rather than at them separately; and reason is no more than that order within the mind which corresponds to the order of the universe. That order itself comes from God; it is the gift, the link that we discussed earlier. God's science, being the cause of everything, is absolutely perfect and noble. Ours, in so far as it is only the effect of things, always remains imperfect, since we always remain short of grasping all the order and all the harmony that prevail in the universe. According to Averroes, "God's science must be called neither specific nor universal. It is the source of all order in the world." That is what the "ancient philosophers" meant when they "insisted that divine intelligence is indeed all intelligences together, all beings, yet in a nobler and more perfect way."

3. In his rejections of Ghazali's objections to philosophers, Averroes shows that he [Ghazali] did not know the philosophers'

ideas through their respective texts, but that he had limited himself
to studying them through their presentation by Avicenna, "hence his
incompetence in the matter," for the philosophers' theses "are based
upon principles that must be discussed first. If we subsequently accept these principles and we recognize the conclusions they claim to
have reached through demonstration, none of these objections against
them is valid any longer." Hence the futility of Ghazali's objections.
Contrary to his claim and according to Averroes, philosophers do
not contest religion, "for it is out of the question, for the philosophers who believe in divinity, to discuss and to polemicize against
the principles of religion. Indeed, since all sciences (the theoretical
ones) are based on proper principles and since he who tackles them
must accept them without questioning their veracity, the same holds
true—and all the more so—for the practical science that is religion."
But Ghazali does not respect this process since he rejects philosophers without "mentioning the motives that had pushed them to
hold their opinions, something that would have allowed the reader
to compare those motives to the discourse to which Ghazali himself
resorted in sullying the philosophers' ideas." This is how "most of
this man's arguments against philosophers are nothing but doubts
that were cast when he contrasted some of their assertions to others,"
and this manner of rejecting is "the most inconsistent and the lowest
that can be, because by no means does it guarantee a consent based
on demonstration or on persuasion."

By contrast with the Ghazalian critique of philosophy, Averroes's
critique of Ash'arism posits the principles and premises upon which
this school bases it doctrine. After thorough examination of these,
Averroes explains that—

> the processes to which the Ash'arites resort to confirm their inter-
> pretations agree with neither the commoners nor the elite, because,
> when examined, they prove unfulfilling to the conditions of dem-
> onstration. (...) Many of the principles upon which the Ash'arites

base their knowledge come from the Sophistic school of thought, because these people deny more than one necessary truth, e.g., the truth of the permanence of accidents, the truth of the influence of things on each another, the truth of the existence of necessary causes to effects, the truth of substantial forms, and the truth of secondary causes. Those of them who did speculate on these questions ended up insulting Muslims since one of the Ash'arite offshoots accuses of infidelity (*kufr*) any one who did not acknowledge the Creator's existence through the methods they had invented in their writings for this purpose...

The main target of Averroes's critique of the Ash'arites was therefore all of the epistemological principles that are at the foundation of their theology, and to which we have eluded earlier:

• the principle of discontinuity and its corollary: the negation of the permanence of accidents;
• the principle of contingency and its corollary: the negation of the existence of necessary causes to effects.

As for the third principle—analogy from the known to the unknown—we have seen Averroes's critique of Avicenna's use of it when reconciling two totally heterogeneous worlds. The Ash'arite method, being based on such principles, cannot possibly attain the rigor of the demonstrative method and becomes as a result unfit for membership by scholars and philosophers. But since it could not even abide by "the obvious data from the dogma that the revealed text meant to urge people to observe," it remains just as unfit to incite the common people. It corrupts the minds of the masses and stirs up the philosophers' opposition. "A careful comparison between the combined Ash'arite principles and the intent of the revealed text shows that on the whole they are nothing but a pile of created assertions, and innovative interpretations."

4. This brings us to the fourth of the major themes that were explored by Averroes: the development of a methodology that makes it possible to "conform to the manifest meaning" of the text. Here Averroes joins Ibn Hazm by developing the *dhahirism* of the latter in such a way that the adopted source of reference is no longer strictly the literalness of the texts, but also "the intention of the revealed text." This expansion was to confer a more rigorously "demonstrative" character unto *dhahirism*. Like Ibn Hazm's, Averroes's method is to abide by the apparent meaning of the revealed text, and not to push interpretation (*ta'wil*)—if this is deemed indispensable—beyond the "semantic shift of an expression from the proper meaning to the figurative," without departing from the Arabic usage. When we are unable to grasp a given meaning, we must resort to the inductive examination of all the revealed text. Averroes adds on top of these elements the necessity to take into consideration the "intention of the revealed text." Following this methodology, Averroes succeeds in establishing that the truths that are attested through the "indicational" way of the revelation and those that are proven through the philosophers' demonstrative method are in agreement and in harmony. "By studying the precious book," he writes, "we shall discover that (the arguments used in the Koran to awaken people to the creation of the world and to the existence of the Creator) are of two sorts:

• firstly, to show the solicitude placed unto man by God, and the fact that all things were created for his sake. We shall call this the "proof by solicitude."

• secondly, to show that God invented the substances of the existing things. He thus invented life unto the (inanimate) bodies as well as sensory perceptions and reason. We shall call this "proof by invention."

This argument, which resorts to "proof by solicitude" and "proof by invention" in order to establish the existence of God, who is accessible to the minds of common people, given the clarity and the simplicity of such proof, and, which agrees with the evidence found in the revelation, since it is the revealed text that suggests it, [such argumentation] "is fundamentally the same as that of the elite (...). The two kinds of knowledge differ only by the amount of details that they provide. The common people are satisfied with knowing solicitude and invention according to a primitive cognitive mode that is based on sensitivity, whereas the scholars add to this knowledge by sensitivity knowledge of solicitude and invention through demonstration. In both cognitive modes, the scholars surpass the common people not only by the amount of their knowledge (i.e., by the amount of details they know), but also by the depth of their knowledge of one and the same thing."

By extending this methodology to the handling of other questions raised by the theologians, we discover, both through the evidence contained in the revelation and through the demonstrative method, that the negation of individual natures of things and the efficiency of causes and the theological understanding of free will and of divine determinism, etc. are but "innovative interpretations" that are devoid of any explicit scriptural support and are not included in the intent of the revealed text. From these considerations, Averroes manages to establish that there is no antagonism or contradiction between wisdom and religion: "Wisdom is the companion and the foster-sister of religion." If one indeed differs from the other in its premises, its principles, and its methods of argumentation, both converge on the same goal: the acquisition of virtue. Both equally aim at truth, and "one truth does not contradict another but is [actually] in agreement with it and testifies in its behalf." Consequently, if an opinion which is attributed to philosophy happens to contradict religion, or if a supposedly religious opinion contradicts philosophy, it must be that "such opinion has no basis in the revelation (as are the theologians opinions on the whole), or that it is an erroneous philosophical opinion, i.e., a false interpretation of philosophy" (like Avicenna's interpretations).

Averroes's philosophical discourse is therefore one of a critical and realistic rationalism. On the cognitive level, Averroes frees himself of the hegemony of the epistemological system sanctioned mostly by the Harran's[27] School in the East and by the neo-platonists in general. Moreover, on the ideological level he frees himself from the socio-historical circumstances that had generated Farabi's dream of the "virtuous city" and Avicenna's "Eastern philosophy." This helped him form a new opinion of the relationship between religion and philosophy, an opinion based on a realistic rationalism that makes it possible to protect the identity and independence of each of these two fields and to make them converge towards the same goal: the search for truth.

The Averroist discourse is a part of the rationalist, realistic and critical discourse of Arab-Islamic thought during the time of the Almohads in the Maghreb and in Al-Andalus. This discourse was itself the reflection of a political struggle, latent at times, overt at others, between the Abbassid and Fatimid caliphates, and the Maghreb and Al-Andalus, which had managed to escape the authority of the Abbassid caliphate since its inception. But a political posture of reserve was intellectually expressed through a critical philosophy. The critical realism of Averroes was not simply the continuation of a trend inaugurated by earlier Andalusian philosophers such as Avempace[28] and Ibn Tufayl. It was rather the fruition of a great critical movement that was permanently driven by a single concern: "to send the East its merchandise back."[29] It is the very same concern that was reflected in the jurisprudence of Ibn Hazm, the *dhahirist*, in the grammar of Ibn Mada',[30] the Cordoban grammarian, in the theology of "Mahdi" Ibn Tumart, and in the philosophy of Averroes.

It was a radically novel conception that Averroes drew of the relationship between religion and philosophy. One must note rationality from within the core of each one of them. Rationality in philosophy is based upon the observance of order and the arrangement of the world and hence upon the principle of causality, whereas rationality in religion is based upon taking into consideration the "legislator's intent," the ultimate finality of which is to incite people to virtue. The notion of "legislator's intent" within the traditional sciences corresponds to that of "natural causes" within the rational sciences. These are the principles upon which Averroes bases his "demonstrationalism." Shatibi[31] and Ibn Khaldun[32] would subsequently come and use the same principles to respectively "put to reason" the revelation and history.

Shatibi and the General Propositions (Kulliyyat) of the Revealed Law (Shari'a)

The two elements of theoretical thinking in Al-Andalus to become distinctive and creative were: (1) systematic and axiomatic vision and (2) the notion of "intentions" as a principle to put to reason an area of thinking where efficient (mechanical) causality is not accepted; the same theoretical thinking which, in its theological and philosophical aspects, had matured under Averroes and was adopted by Shatibi in his attempt at rethinking the basis of the sources/foundations of jurisprudence.

In jurisprudence, how do we base rationality on the "categorical" (*qat'*)—which is the equivalent of "certainty" in the rational sciences—when we know that this science is based on transmission (*naql*) and does not derive from reason? It is quite possible, Shatibi assures us, provided we use the demonstrative method and base the foundations/sources on the "general propositions of the law" and on the "the legislator's intentions." The "general propositions" of the law are the equivalent of the "rational propositions" of the theoretical sciences. As for the intentions of the legislator, they represent the "final cause" that regulates the rationality of the law.

This is fine; but how do we arrive at "general propositions" in the law, knowing that the law is made up of injunctions and proscriptions having to do with specific cases? We arrive at these general propositions the same way we would in the theoretical sciences, Shatibi replies: through examination (*istiqra*) of all of the specific propositions of the law, from which we would infer the general propositions. To be sure, these general propositions would be derived from induction by enumeration,[33] but nonetheless they remain categorical, just like the "general propositions of the Arabic language," i.e., grammar rules, and the propositions of the other inductive sciences similar to grammar.

The general propositions of the law are categorical designations because the inductive procedure they derive from is subject to the same criteria as in the demonstrative sciences. There are, according to Shatibi, three such instances:

(1) Universality and generality. Legal prescriptions in fact possess these two qualities since they apply to all responsible humans vis-à-vis the law (*mukallafun*) and since their application is not restricted to a given time or place.

(2) Permanence and immutability. Legal prescriptions are indeed permanent and immutable: what is prescribed as imperative (*wajib*) remains so; what is prescribed as prohibited (*haram*) remains so, also. What is given as cause (*sabab*) remains a cause; what is given as condition[34] (*shart*) remains a condition.

(3) Sovereignty, i.e., "in the case of a science, the fact of being absolutely judging but not subject to judgment." The law is indeed made up of injunctions and proscriptions over which no authority can prevail. The law thus fulfills the conditions of a demonstrative science and, though "given" rather than produced by reason,

> it is the equal of the rational sciences in as much as it dispenses a categorical knowledge (...). For science, within the sphere of Jurisprudence, is an examination that re-arranges spread-out elements in such a way that these elements appear to reason as a set of universal general propositions that are not null-and-void and

not obsolete, that are judging but not subject to judgment. These are also the characteristics of the rational general propositions. The latter are inferred from an examination whose object is the universe, and this universe is a "given" thing, not a construction of reason. From this viewpoint the rational general propositions in no way differ from the general propositions of the law.

For Shatibi, these are the general propositions of the law, or the premises of the demonstrative procedure with regard to the science of the sources/foundations of jurisprudence. As for the "legislator's intentions," which are pendants of causality in matters of law, Shatibi notes four major ones:

(1) Protecting the interests of humanity. These interests are of three kinds: vital, utilitarian and superfluous. The human being has five vital interests: self-preservation, and the protection of his mental health, of his species, of his property and of his religion. The utilitarian interests, such as clothing, housing, etc., cannot be completely delineated. As for the superfluous, it varies to the extreme: perfume, luxury clothing, domestic luxury, etc.;

(2) Communicating. The law is meant to be understood. In order to understand this law, which was revealed in the language and culture of the Arabs, we must go back to the socio-linguistic practices [rules] of Arab society;

(3) Determining the obligations. The general rule here says that "from a legal point of view, man ought not to be forced into an action of which he is incapable, even if this were rationally possible," for "God only imposes on each man what he can bear."[35]

(4) "To shield the responsible man—vis-à-vis the divine law—from the urges of his passions so that he can be a servant of God by his free choice as he is by necessity."

Such are the "intentions" to take into consideration when determining a legal designation. Since there are four of them, are these "intentions" not comparable to Aristotle's four "causes"? Could we not relate the "material cause" to the "capacity to fulfill ones obligations"; the "formal cause" to the "the practices of the Arabs"; the "efficient cause" to the "intention to shield man from the grip of his passions"; and the "final cause" to "the interest of men"? In the least, let us say that the rationality model, recognized by reference in the demonstrative method during the medieval period, was an Aristotelian model. It is therefore not surprising to note traces of this model in all the projects which attempted to put to reason different systems of thinking, be they purely theoretical systems, e.g., the rational sciences (Averroes), or sciences that are inscribed within a rational framework, e.g., the science of the foundations/sources of jurisprudence (Shatibi) or the interpretation of history (Ibn Khaldun).

Ibn Khaldun and the "Natural Properties of Civilization" (Tabba'i' al-'umran)

In the introduction to his *Prolegomena*, Ibn Khaldun explains that having read the historians' works and noticed how these were full of accounts that related unreasonable facts as presented, he decided to write his own history book which he describes as follows:

> Thanks to this book I have lifted the veil on the conditions for the emergence of generations, and have divided it in chapters dealing with historical accounts as well as with the meaning of events. In it, I have explained the causes that are inherent to the genesis of civilization and of dynasties (...). In short, it is a commentary on the conditions of civilization and urbanization (*tamaddun*), on the appropriate characteristics of people living in society. This commentary lets the reader enjoy the knowledge of the causes of birth and evolution of civilization feats and understand how dynasty founders established their power.

We see plainly that we are dealing here with a project that makes it history's turn to become a science based on demonstration. It elevates history, which was once no more than an exercise in compiling "accounts about wars and dynasties, as well as about the earliest centuries, with so many exaggerations that people enjoyed quoting as examples," to the rank of a scientific practice based on "rigorous examination of accounts, explanation of deeds and their genesis through causality and deep knowledge of the 'how' and 'why' of facts." Thus conceived, history was to become a part of the demonstrative sciences: "It has its basis and its roots within wisdom (philosophy) and fully deserves to be counted as one of these sciences."

How does one make a science out of history when the object of history is the relating of specific facts that are punctual, are inscribed within specific temporal and spatial conditions, having, each, their own immediate and remote causes? Ibn Khaldun replies that if history is indeed made up of a series of "accounts of events," which are specific facts, it is no less feasible to take the first step to an approach that is capable of raising history into a science. It is possible if we succeed in getting the account to comply with reality so that the account no longer tells us simply about the temporal and spatial situation of the reported event, but also about the causes that made it possible, and that it [the account] represents the event for us in a rational intelligible form.

Accordingly, the priority task of the historian who wants to make history scientific is to develop an "exact criterion" according to which he would evaluate the reported accounts and distinguish those that are in compliance with reality and those that are not. This criterion lies in the knowledge of the "natural properties of civilization." Indeed, "civilization" (*'umran*), in its various conditions, possesses natural properties (*tabāʾiʿ*), to which accounts must be brought back and in terms of which the related traditions (*riwayat*) and the words of the ancient ones (*athar*) must be appreciated." We would not therefore be able to put history into reason, i.e., to submit to rational consistency the representation of reality which is offered by the accounts, unless we "knew the natural properties of civilization." This is "the safest path for the examination of the reported accounts and for the distinction between the true and the false. It comes before the examination whose method is the critique of recorders.[36] We should not resort to this critique until we have established that the account is in itself possible or impossible. If it is impossible, there is no need whatsoever to proceed to the recorders' critique." In other words, "The rule to apply in distinguishing the true from the false in these accounts, working from the notions of possibility and impossibility, is to examine human society, that is civilization. To do that, we must note from its midst: the conditions that affect it from its essence and according to its nature; those that affect it by accident and ought not to be considered, and those that cannot affect it. Within the science of human society, "The natural properties of civilization" are therefore "general propositions." Since events take place by virtue of a nature that is proper to civilization and they are thus necessary, they are governed by the principle of causality, just like all other created things: "Every thing created in the mundane world, be it essence or an animal or human act, necessarily requires a cause that precedes it, thanks to which it becomes inscribed in the "permanence of habit"[37] and reaches its conclusion. I am talking here about causes that reason can determine, those through which reason establishes the rationale of things. These are the "apparent natural causes for which reason—after perceiving them—must specify the order and the disposition." As for the metaphysical and the "invisible" causes, such as intentions and human will, these are psychic phenomena that cannot be subject to causal knowledge.

Yet, some events that pertain to natural properties of civilization and that are intrinsically linked to it are to a certain extent determined by the revealed law. Must we exclude them from rationality and assign them to the "invisible causes," or must we all the same ascribe to them their own rationality? Ibn Khaldun answers this question in Averroist terms. He justifies the legal prescriptions having to do with civilization, with government and with the state apparatus by the fact that they proceed from the "legislator's intention." Their rationality resides in that they proceed from the consideration of the common good (*maslaha*). Thus, for example, the legislator imposed the "Quraysh extraction" as a condition for accession to the caliphate only because the most appropriate "tribal solidarity" (*'asabiyya*) that guarantees the preponderance of one people over the others during the prophet's era was that of Quraysh.

If it is understood that "birth among Quraysh" was placed as a condition for accession to the caliphate to avoid conflicts, because of their (Quraysh) "tribal solidarity" and their preponderance, and that the legislator does not promulgate specific laws for one single generation, single era or single nation, we would soon realize that such clause is about competence (*kifaya*).[38] We therefore connect the two and we generalize the application of the motive which justified the requirement of the Quraysh-extraction: tribal solidarity. Accordingly, we find it necessary that he who is in charge of the affairs of the Muslims belong to a group whose tribal solidarity is the strongest and superior to that of its contemporaries, so that this group may force the others to follow it and so that the general unification allow for an efficacious defense.

And so willed the natural properties of civilization: "what is happening in the world confirms what we are saying. Only he who rises highest over a nation or a people is capable of running its affairs." Here, the divine prescription itself is thus in agreement with the natural properties of civilization. Indeed, "It is quite rare that the divine order run counter to the order of the world."

This epistemological overview of philosophical thought in Arab-Islamic society has revealed to us two distinct moments in the history of consciousness of this society. The first of these moments had the emanationist-metaphysics apparatus as an epistemological foundation, and the fusion of religion and philosophy as an ideological basis. This moment was dominated by an idealist and spiritualist vision, which led the social forces of progress to sublimate in dream their incapacity to achieve their aspirations. The second moment was epistemological, inaugurated by the critical contributions of Ibn Hazm and Ibn Tumart. Ideologically, it was inaugurated by the course of the political conflict between the Abbassid caliphate, which promoted a thinking where the temporal turns absolute inside religion, and a Maghrebian-Andalusian state whose very existence was proof that plurality of the "temporal" could [co]exist within religious unity.

This is the deep significance of the problematics posed by philosophical thought in Islam, both East and West. Philosophy therefore, has never been an imported object or a foreign body within the Arab-Islamic society, but the expression of a native experience. Philosophy reflected society's problems and sufferings and was the mouthpiece of its hopes and dreams. It was indeed its consciousness.

---

[1]Al-Andalus became an independent entity as early as 138/755, the date when the "Emigrant" 'Abd al-Rahman al-Dakhil, an offspring from the Omeyyad family, having escaped the massacre against his relatives by the newly established Abbassid regime, took refuge in Andalusia where he founded the Omeyyad Emirate of Al-Andalus. The Fatimid dynasty was founded by 'Abdallah or 'Ubayddallah, a supposed descendant of the Isma'ilian lineage—and recognized by these as "Mahdi"—who arrived in the land known these days as Tunisia and managed to overthrow the Aghlabid regime in 297/910. The Fatimids later moved their capital to Cairo where their caliphate became a political threat to both the Abbassid Caliphate and the Omeyyad state in Al-Andalus for a long time.

[2] A historian, born in Almeria (420-462/1029-1070), who held the position of Malikite judge (*qadi*) in Toledo. He is known for his *Tabaqat al-Umram*, a great history text on nations and civilizations.

[3] That is to say under the reign of 'Abd al-Rahman III, eighth Omeyyad Emir who, after putting an end to the internal strife inside al-Andalus and pushing away the Christian threat, installed the Omeyyad Caliphate in Cordoba in 316/928.

⁴ Within the terminology used by hadith scholars, this word refers to those protectors of hadith who had lived during the time of the Prophet's companions (*sahaba*), not having known the Prophet personally.

⁵ A school of theology founded by Abu al-Hasan al-Ash'ari (260-324/873-935). Following the failure of Mu'tazilism in Baghdad, this Mu'tazilite defector sought to initiate a "middle way" between the traditionalism represented by the Hanbalite school and the practice of dialectical theology. His school was thus able to become the predominant school of theology in the Abbassid empire. Among the most notable representatives of this school worth mentioning are Baqillani (fourth-fifth/tenth-eleventh centuries), Juwayni (fifth/eleventh century) who was Ghazali's master, and Shahrastani, Ghazali's contemporary. No matter what differences they may have had, all trends of Ash'arism had in common: a) the affirmation of the uncreated Qur'an, b) the affirmation of the inaccessibility of God's mystery as well as the reality of the divine attributes, c) the absolute preeminence of the law, d) the negation of the ontological reality of secondary causes, and e) the negation of human free will.

⁶ Originally from Baa'lbek, the founder of this school (*madhhab*) had lived in Damascus where he received the protection of the last Omeyyad caliphs. He died in 157/774. The Abbassids allowed the Awza'ite school to remain in Syria and its last Mufti died in Damascus in 347/958.

⁷ In the Arab East, at the beginning of the Abbassid era, the drafting of Muslim law, Shari'a, was the work of three groups that were associated with distinct regions: an Iraqi group that followed Abu Hanifa (died 150/767), and later became the Hanafite School (*madhhab*); a group from Medina that followed Malik Ibn Anas (died 179/795), the founder of the Malikite School; and a Syrian group following Awza'i (cf. preceding note) with a short-lived influence. The juridical practice of the Hanafiite tradition insists on the use of "personal judgment" (*ra'y*) and upon the finalization of such judgment by a search for the best "preferential judgment" (*istihsan*). The decision thus formulated must have, as a base, the expansion of the third source of jurisprudence, analogical reasoning (*qiyass*), besides the book (Qur'an) and the tradition (hadith). The Malikite School attaches importance both to consensus (*ijma'*) and to personal judgment (*ra'y*) of the scholars. It is the School that takes account the most of customary law (*'urf*), namely the "customary law of Medina" at the time of Malik. The subsequent strict codification of jurisprudence (*fiqh*) and of the notion of foundations/sources of the law (*usul al-Fiqh*) was proposed by Muhammad Ibn Idris al-Shafi'i (150-204/767-820). He presented in his famous *Risala* (Epistle) the principles of a juridical methodology according to which judgment (*hukm*) had to be drawn, by order of priority, from the book (the Qur'an), tradition (hadith), analogical reasoning (*qiyas*), or from *consensus doctorum* (*ijma'*). Thus al-Shafi'i was the founder of a third established juridical school. But the methodological principles that he put forth had a

considerable influence on the subsequent evolution of the two preceding schools. Besides these schools, there persisted a traditionalist legal attitude that was hostile to both the Shafi'ites and their reasoned conciliation of tradition and consensus and the schools of Iraq and Medina. Starting in the third/ninth century, these legal attitudes led to the establishment of a legislative structure made up of compilations by Ibn Hanbal, the great hadith scholar. Hanbalism later became recognized as the fourth "official" juridical school in the Sunni world.

[8] Which means "esoterists." *Batin* (latent) refers to the esoteric aspect of the revelation, as opposed to the *dhahir* (manifest) exoteric aspect. It is particularly true of the Isma'ilian denomination at the time of the Fatimids.

[9] Cf. note 6 of Chapter 4.

[10] Abu Bakr Muhammad Ibn 'abd al-Malik Ibn Tufayl (died 580/1185) was born in Guadix (*wadi 'akh*), northeast of Granada, Andalusia. He studied medicine and philosophy in Seville and Cordoba and was introduced to Abu Ya'qub Yusuf, the Almohad Caliph, to whom he introduced Averroes. Of all his works, the only one that made it to posterity is *Hayy Ibn Yaqdhan* (*Vivens filius vigilantis*), a Roman allegorical novel titled after an esoteric text by Avicenna.

[11] Cf. note 5.

[12] One of the Greek works that exerted a most decisive influence on Arab philosophical thinking was a book known under the name of *Aristotle's Theology*, which is actually a neoplatonist text, a paraphrase of Plotinus' Books IV, V and VI of the *Enneads*, often attributed to Proclusius. The emanationist conceptions presented in this supposedly Aristotelian work were of great help to those, like al-Farabi, who sought to reconcile Plato's doctrine and that of Aristotle.

[13] Cf. note 6 of Chapter 2.

[14] Al-Murabitun, a Berber dynasty of Saharan origin, which unified the Moroccan regions and the western part of the central Maghreb between 448/1056 and 475/1082, in the name of an intransigent Malikite doctrine. Marrakesh, founded in 454/1062, was its capital. In 483/1090 some of the rulers that had divided the Andalusian territory after the fall of the Omeyyad dynasty in 420/1031 called on Yusuf Ibn Tashfin, the Almoravid leader, to help push back the advance of the *Reconquista* launched by Alphonse of Castille. The Almoravids then took over Al-Andalus, thus ending the era of the "Kings of Taifas" (*muluk al-Tawa'if*). The Almoravid rule remained in place until 541/1147.

[15] Al-Muwahidun, a dynasty born from the insurrection movement of a religious reform launched by Muhammad Ibn Tumart, known as the "Mahdi" (died 524/1130), which put an end to the Almoravid rule in 541/1147. Their rule, under the reigns of Abu Ya'qub Yusuf (558-580/1163-1184) and of his son Ya'qub al-Mansur (580-595/1163-1184), extended over the whole of North Africa, all the

way to the borders of Egypt. The advent of the Marinids in Marrakesh put an end to their dynasty in 668/1269.

[16] Abu Muhammad 'Ali Ibn Hazm (384-456/994-1063) was born in Cordoba where his father was vizier to the regent chamberlain al-Mansur Ibn Abi 'Amir. He benefited from the teachings of some of Cordoba's most famous masters in all disciplines: science of hadith, history, philosophy, jurisprudence, medicine, literature (adab). Following some political unrest that was linked to the decline of the Omeyyad rule, he was expelled from Cordoba. He then took refuge in Almeria where he headed a movement in favor of prince 'Abd al-Rahman IV, legitimate pretender to the caliphate. He always remained faithful to the Omeyyad cause. Ibn Hazm's most important work was his treatise on religions and the schools of thought, called *Kitab al-Fisal fi al-milal wa al-ahwa' wa al-nihal*. In terms of jurisprudence, he adopted the *dhahirist* or "exoterist" doctrine founded in the East by Dawud al-Isfahani (died 270/884), which was devoted to the validation of the letter of the text (the Qur'an), i.e., of the "manifest" (*dhahir*). Ibn Hazm took advantage of this doctrine to condemn juridical analogy (*qiyas*) and to base juridical reasoning upon strict demonstrative principles.

[17] Cf. preceding note.

[18] Regarding the notions of "indication" (*bayan*), "demonstration" (*burhan*) and "illumination" (*'irfan*) as defined by M.A. al-Jabri, see his work, *Naqd al 'aql al-'Arabi*.

[19] See preceding note.

[20] A Mu'tazilite theologian from Basra (died 235/850).

[21] To defend the notion of the divine all-mightiness, Muslim theologians in general denied the notion of causality inherent in things and explained the recurrence of natural phenomena by the notion of "habit" (*'ada*) that is established by God but which He theoretically could break at any moment; hence the notion of "breaking the habit" (*Kharq al-'ada*).

[22] Sufyan al-Thawri (died 161/778) was a great hadith scholar (*muhaddith*) and the founder of a jurisprudence school of traditionalist inspiration in Kufa. The last *mufti* from this school died in Baghdad in 405/1015.

[23] For the Isma'ilians of the Fatimid era, the imam and caliph, being in a privileged relationship with the afterlife, was supposed to state an absolute truth, and his teaching (*ta'lim*) was infallible

[24] *Al-amr bi al-ma'ruf wa al-nahy 'an al-munkar* was the obligation of all Muslims as stated in the Qur'an (cf. Qur'an III, 104 and IX 71). This principle was the subject of various interpretations among theologians as to the question of knowing if it had to be accomplished "by the hand," "by the tongue," or "by the heart"; if it was the sole responsibility of the political leader or any believer, etc. In its

maximalist interpretation, it was likely to become a political argument lending credence to the idea that it was necessary to overthrow the guilty leaders or to force the opponents to adopt a "true doctrine."

[25] Averroes is the author of a refutation of Ghazali's *Tahafut al-Falasifa* (The Incoherence of Philosophers) , which he called *Tahafut al-Tahafut* (The Incoherence of Incoherence).

[26] *Al-Kashf 'an manahij al-'adilla fi 'aqa'id al-milla* is the title of a treatise by Averroes whose topic was defined by the author as "the study of the apparent meaning (*dhahir*) of the dogma to which the legislator wanted the common people to subscribe," as distinct from the false beliefs into which the theologians' unfounded interpretations had thrown them.

[27] The "Sabeans" of the city of Harran were a religious community that had settled in northern Mesopotamia at an early time. From what we know of their religious tradition, the Harranians recognize the prophecy of Agathodemon and Hermes— likened to Seth and Idris—and that of Orpheus. They believed in the existence of a transcendent creator, accessible only by way of interceding spirits—whose intelligences dwelt in the spheres of the seven planets—to whose reality the purified human soul could have access. Though this community had long struggled for survival under Muslim rule, it gave the Arab-Islamic civilization many eminent scholars. Their scientific heritage was one of the means used by the Hermetist tradition to infiltrate Arab-Islamic civilization.

[28] Abu Bakr Muhammad Ibn Yahya Ibn al-Sa'igh Ibn Bajja, whom the Latins called Avempace (died 533/1138). He was born in Saragossa at the end of the fifth/ eleventh century, but had to take refuge in Seville after his home town was taken by Alphonse I of Aragon. He practiced medicine there as well as in Granada. He was later poisoned by his physician-colleagues in the court of Fes. He was one the first great names in philosophy in Al-Andalus during the Almoravid rule. He is known for his commentaries on some of Aristotle's treatises (e.g., physics, meteorology, history of animals). The majority of his writings remained unfinished. The treatise that earned him fame is the *Tadbir al-mutawahhid* (The Regimen of the Recluse). He paved a new path for philosophy in Al-Andalus, and this was to become fully articulated through the work of Averroes.

[29] A reference to a famous sentence by the Buyid Vizier Sahib Ibn 'Abbad, a great Eastern patron of letters, who, after reading the literary anthology of an Andalusian author, Ibn 'Abd Rabbih, one day made the remark: "It is our [own] merchandise that they are sending [us] back!"

[30] Ahmad Ibn 'Abd al-Rahman Ibn Muhammad Ibn Mada' (513-592/1119-1195). As a great grammarian from Cordoba, he was mostly known for his *Kitab al-Radd 'ala al-Nuhat* (The Refutation of Grammarians). In it, Ibn Mada' critiques the

principle of motivation (*ta'lil*) of the Arabic (inflectional) case endings. The theories of the Eastern grammarians stated, indeed, that verbs and nouns in Arabic sentences were affected by such inflection because of their syntactic function, considered as the "motive" (*'illa*) of the inflection in question. We can see the affinities of this approach with that of the jurists (the Shafi'ites in particular), for whom the juridical designations had to also have a motive. For example, the motive for the prohibition of alcohol was its "inebriating feature" *(iskar)*, by virtue of which the designation of prohibition could be extended to any drink that shared the same feature. Ibn Mada' therefore thought that grammatical phenomena could not be explained, and should be simply noted and deduced from linguistic data.

[31] Abu Ishaq Ibn Musa al-Shatibi (died 790/1388), a native of Granada, was an Andalusian jurist. His education combined both the traditional and the rational sciences. He is the author of *Kitab al-I'tisam*, a treatise against heresies and *Muwafaqat fi usul al-Shari'a*, a crucial treatise on the science of the foundations/ sources of jurisprudence. Living in a period of cultural decline in Al-Andalus, he painfully experienced the social and intellectual situation of his time, e.g., omnipresence of brotherhood-Sufism, and predominance of "imitative conformism" (*taqlid*) in jurisprudence matters. This state of affairs must have greatly influenced his reform project of rebasing the sources/foundations of jurisprudence on the "legislator's intentions" (*maqasid*)', i.e., the common good, a pendant of Aristotle's "final cause" (good), which Shatibii, along the lines of Averroes, wanted to substitute for the old principle of juridical analogy. Although Shatibi's project had remained ineffective because of the general decline of Al-Andalus during that time, his juridical thinking remained nonetheless prevalent throughout the whole Maghreb. Muhammad 'Abduh, who held him in high esteem, knew the *Muwafaqat* and the *I'tisam* from a sojourn he made in Tunisia. More recently, 'Allal al-Fasi, a Moroccan Salafi reformer and politician, had espoused Shatibi's views.

[32] 'Abd al-Rahman Muhammad Ibn Khaldun (732-808/1332-1406) was born in Tunis into an Andalusian family of scholars and civil servants. There he studied the Qur'anic sciences, linguistics, hadith and jurisprudence. In 753/1352 he settled in the court of Abu 'Inan, the Marinid Sultan, in Fes. It was there that he became acquainted with Avicenna's and Averroes's thinking. He frequented various political centers throughout the Maghreb and Al-Andalus before retiring, in 776/1375, to write his most important work, the *Muqaddima*, which was the introduction to his *Kitab al-'Ibar* (History of the World). He entered the employ of the Mameluk Sultan of Egypt where he became Supreme (Malikite) Judge. In his *Muqaddima*, he lay the principles of a new independent science to be defined by its very target: the whole of human civilization. He distinguished himself through a critique of the Islamic historiography and proposed a method for verifying historical data based on laws that are inherent to history. The great originality of his conceptions

led some to credit him for being the founder of critical history and precursor of modern sociology.

[33] Induction by enumeration, synonymous with formal induction, is the operation through which one enumerates the different species which make up a genre, in order to infer a proposition related to the latter. In Shatibi's juridical perspective, this amounts to enumerating all the specific prescriptions drawn from the juridical sources (the Qur'an and the hadith) about a given point in order to infer (from them) a general proposition. From a logical point of view, this mode of reasoning is perfectly rigorous and conclusive, provided the number of cases in question is finite and completely enumerated, which is obviously the case in Shatibi's method. This is what entitles one to believe that the general propositions of the law, though "inferred from induction by enumeration," are *categorical*.

[34] Within the terminology related to the science of the foundations/sources of jurisprudence, "cause" and "condition" are modalities that affect certain facts and justify the juridical designations of these. We would say, for example, that a "hardship circumstance" is the "cause" by virtue of which eating the meat of a dead animal becomes permissible; and that an orphan's coming of age (i.e., reaching majority) is the "condition" upon which it becomes mandatory for a guardian to remit to that orphan his savings (estate).

[35] Qur'an, II 286.

[36] A method of external critique used by Muslim scholars within the traditional sciences and especially codified in its application to the science of hadith. It consists in checking the transmitted data (*khabar*) by examining the chain of recorders (*isnad*) through whom such data has reached us. Two major criteria must be considered: *continuity* of the chain, which guarantees that the information was indeed transmitted from the source to destination without interruption; and *credibility* of the recorders who [would] guarantee the veracity of the transmitted data. To this end, the critique goes on to the vindication (*ta'dil*) or the defamation (*tajrih*) of each recorder, using mostly the criterion of morality. This method was to remain almost the only approach of criticism to be used by historians in the Arab-Islamic context, something Ibn Khaldun reproached them for as he rejected this external criterion of validity for what relates to data concerning facts (*waqi'at*), "the veracity of which depended exclusively on their compliance (*mutabaqa*) with the outside world." (Ibn Khaldun, *Al-Muqaddima*, ed. Dar al-Jiil, Beirut, s.d., p. 41).

[37] For Ibn Khaldun, who re-uses, within this context, a formula by Baqillani (died 403/1013), the Ash'arite theologian from Baghdad, "habit" (*'ada*) has not been "broken" since the end of the prophecy-era, during which time miracles could still happen. The recurrence of events from the natural and human world is therefore totally guaranteed, which makes of the natural properties of civilization a possible science.

[38] Mawardi (died 450/1058), a Shafi'ite jurist from Baghdad, had presented—at the behest of Caliph al-Qadir—in a treatise that became a classic the position of his school regarding public law. He had enacted seven conditions for accession to the function of caliph, to which he added the "Quraysh extraction." Ibn Khaldun, for his part, brings down these conditions to four points: science (*'ilm*); honorable record (*'adala*); soundness of sight and of hearing and lack of physical disabilities; and competence (*kifaya*), defined as the courage and the necessary strength to protect the state (cf. Al-Muqaddima, p. 213). While Mawardi, by positing the requirement of the Quraysh-extraction, sought to justify the existing régime, i.e., the Abbassids, Ibn Khaldun reduced this prescription to the requirement of "competence," thus inscribing it within the laws of the history he wanted to create.

Conclusion
The Future Can Only Be Averroist

Human thought is an uninterrupted dialogue between the past and the present, between the present and the future. Any "solution" to the problems of the past, on the theoretical level, implies the knowledge of how to resolve, on the "practical" level, those of the present and the future. We have addressed the question of the relationship of our ancestors to Greek philosophy. But how do we today define our relationship to our ancestors' philosophy, i.e., the Arab-Islamic philosophy?

This question takes us back to the initial problem: the search for a workable method to assume our relationship to *tradition*. In the first part of this essay, we discussed the problem at the level of method and of vision, i.e., the understanding of our *tradition* that we needed to construct for ourselves. We must now pose the problem anew, but at the level of "theoretical practice," that is to say the investment of tradition in our intellectual activity today.

It goes without saying that these two aspects are linked: the type of understanding of tradition that we construct will directly determine the type of investment that we will make of it. Similarly, the function that we would want to ascribe to it will in turn affect the way we construct our conception. Yet, there are limits beyond which we cannot go in this investment process. What we can invest in today's intellectual activity is not *tradition* as a whole but rather tradition as survival. Let us then ask ourselves what has survived from the Arab-Islamic philosophy.

Problems are never more complicated and more abstruse than when they are ill-posed. Contemporary Arab thought, for which the problem of the relationship to tradition has always been an essential element, has never been able to go beyond this problematics because it has always ill-posed the problems that are associated with it.

To pose the problem of the relationship to tradition while asking "what there would be to take or to leave" from this totality which is tradition, as a body of knowledge, of information, of ideas, of debates, of interpretations that are consigned in the ancient books, printed or handwritten, is an erroneous approach, lacking in objectivity and in historical perspective. For tradition is not a merchandise produced at once, outside of history. It is indeed a part of history and it is thought in motion made up of thought momentums at given stages of its development. It is thus made-up of successive moments that eliminate or complement each other; moments of thought that reflect a reality, express it and act upon it, positively or negatively. The scientific treatment of tradition must hence operate on two levels: understanding and investing. On the first level, we must effectively ensure that we can assimilate our tradition as a whole, in its diverse trends and throughout its historical stages. On the investing level, however, we must concentrate more on the highest moment of its progress. To wonder what there is to borrow from the Mu'tazilites, the Shi'ites, the Kharijites, the Ash'arites or the philosophers is an ahistorical attitude that locks those who adopt it inside their own vicious circles. The gains from tradition with which we want to interact—perhaps the only ones with which interaction is possible today—are not the ones our ancestors experienced, which are currently preserved in books, but rather what has survived from them, i.e., that which can still answer some of our present concerns and can be developed and enriched so as to take us into the future... Authenticity (*asala*) for us is just that.

But what has survived from our tradition?

It is no longer that difficult to clearly answer this question after our discussion of the components of our philosophical tradition, which enabled us to emphasize the need to distinguish between the cognitive and the ideological contents. The cognitive content of Islamic philosophy, like that of any philosophy from before the contemporary era, is in a large part a dead subject incapable of reviving. It is a different matter for the ideological content, which is capable of having "another life" that goes on throughout the ages, in different forms. The cognitive content of a philosophy, no matter which one, lives only once, then dies forever, without any hope of resuscitation. Moslem philosophers, like all medieval philosophers, founded their philosophy upon the physical sciences of Aristotle. The cognitive content of this entire philosophy collapsed with the advent of modern science. Descartes thus founded his philosophy upon Galileo's physics, to the shaping of which he had himself contributed. But the cognitive content of Cartesianism ceased to be operational with the advent of Newton's physics. Then Kant founded his own philosophy upon the latter, which philosophy became in turn outdated when Newtonian physics became outdated with the advent of the quantum theory, the theory of relativity, etc. The cognitive content is science and science has its history. Yet, the history of science is, as Bachelard said, the history of the errors of science. That is why the cognitive content of any philosophy dies once and for all, and forever: because it enters history as a sum of "errors." It collapses and dies without hope of resuscitation, because error has no history.

It is quite another thing for the ideological content of philosophy: it is in itself an ideology, and the time of ideology is the "possible-future," a future which ideology lives in the present, but in the form of a dream. By nature, dreams ignore the parameters of space and time, contrary to science, whose time is the "current present," which it [science] lives in its present. When its present expires, it eliminates itself to be born again in a new current present. This is why we, people of the twentieth century, can be in agreement with certain ideological aspirations of philosophers from the past, but not necessarily with the cognitive subject matter they brought into play in their philosophy. This subject matter disturbs us and prevents us from adhering to their discourse, ideologically and philosophically.

Conclusion

After these theoretical considerations, let us analyze the ideo-logical content of the Arab-Islamic philosophy, in order to establish the distinction between what is permanently dead within this content and what is likely to relive "another life." We previously stated that the time of ideology was the "possible future," having placed the future between quotations marks. Now, we must lift the siege from around this future. The future of ideology is not univocal: there are ideologies that live their "future" (their dream) in the past; and others that live it in the time to-come. Only the latter ideology is likely to experience another life, because it is in itself a momentum toward this life.

How do we differentiate between these two types?

Here again, we must call upon historical vision and historical consciousness. Tradition is an integral part of history and, hence, of historical "becoming". If we previously stressed the fact that only the ideological content had a history—to the exclusion of the cognitive one—, it is because the ideological content partakes of the process of society's evolution. Thus in general, it reflects "becoming" upon the specific domain of thought, which will consequently acquire its own autonomy of "becoming," its own process of eliminating past moments by subsequent ones. Therefore, an ideology living its "future" in the past is an ideology still living one of those moments already eliminated by the process of a "becoming" that is specific to the thinking with which this ideology is associated. On the other hand, an ideology that aims its future toward the time-to-come is one that lives one or several moments not yet eliminated by the process of "becoming."

As we consider our philosophical tradition in light of these re-marks, it will be easy to recognize what has survived from it. Having irrevocably discarded its cognitive content, let us now consider "be-coming" from its ideological content. We noted two moments for such "becoming", the second one having eliminated the first and broken with it. The first moment is that of al-Farabi's dream experienced by Avicenna in his own way. The second moment, expanded by Averroes,[1] is that of Avempace's dream. What survives from our tradition cannot possibly be associated with the first moment, since the latter was historically eliminated by the second moment. It is history which tells all this. Hence, any person having lived, or still living, the Avicennian moment after the advent of Averroes is condemned to live intellectually on the margin of history. Consequently, we, post-Averroes Arabs, have lived on the margin of history (in inertia and decline), because we kept clinging to the Avicennian moment after Ghazali granted it currency within "Islam." As for Europeans, they went on to live the very history that we had exited, because they knew how to appropriate Averroes and how to keep living the Averroes moment to this day.

The survival of our philosophical tradition, i.e., what is likely to contribute to our time, can only be Averroist. Let us examine then in the following passages the remnants of Averroism that are likely to be invested in our intellectual activity today.

1. Averroism entered history because it broke with that Avicennianism of "oriental" philosophy that Avicenna himself had chosen and that was then adopted partly by Ghazali and partly by Suhrawardi of Aleppo. The scholars and jurisconsults who firmly espoused Islam's original character, its Arab character, always rejected Sufism, in which they saw a foreign commodity imported from Persia and incompatible with the Muslim religion, which was based on a simple and spontaneous belief. When Avicenna reconstructed the pagan-based Harranian emanationist metaphysics, and coated it with an Islamic varnish, Ghazali borrowed it from him to make of it an alternative to Aristotelian philosophy. But as a partisan of the Ash'arite doctrine, Ghazali spread this Avicennian "oriental" commodity as "Sunni Sufism." That was an incoherent and contradictory appellation since the notion of Sufism was absent from the hadith. The Prophet never was a mystic; instead, he lived a normal life, and the

norms upon which Islam was based during his time were by no means in favor of "gloom" or esoterism, but rather in favor of a reasonable realism. The discourse of the Koran was one of reason and not one of "gnosticism" or illuminism.

Averroes knew how to break with Avicenna. Therefore, let us borrow this "rupture" from him—since one has to use this word— and in turn break with Avicenna's gnostic spirit decisively and definitively, and launch a decisive battle against it.

2. Averroes not only broke with the Avicennian and gnostic spirit. He also broke with the manner in which theoretical thinking—both theological and philosophical—had addressed the critical relationship between religion and philosophy. He rejected the theologians' way of reconciling between reason and transmission, just as he rejected the way of the philosophers who sought the fusion of religion into philosophy and vice versa.

Why is that?

Because the theologians had appropriated the hereafter (religion) to their segmentarist-atomist reason, and from that conception of religion that they had constructed, they fashioned for themselves a certain idea of reason. Hence, they conceived the invisible world by analogy with the tangible world. As a result, they produced innovative interpretations and projected on the tangible world elements that allowed them to produce analogies with their idea of the invisible world, thus distorting reality and obstructing the activity of reason.

Philosophers had appropriated religion to "science"—represented during their time by the metaphysical cognitive legacy of Greece— and they had reduced science to the conception of religion that they had constructed for themselves. They had thus narrowed science down to the level of their understanding of religion, instead of making the latter evolve in tandem with scientific evolution.

Averroes broke with that conception of the relationship between religion and science and the one between religion and philosophy. Let us then reconsummate this break—since we definitely have to use the term—and let us cease wanting to explain religion through science and abusively link one to the other; because science is in constant mutation, incessantly contradicting and surpassing itself. And let us by the same token cease wanting to subordinate science to religion. Science needs no external restrictions whatsoever because it sets its own limits for itself.

3. Averroes did not limit himself to "rupture." He also offered the possibility of a "carry-on spirit." Rupture—the way we mean it herein—comes about only through efforts to carry-on with a spirit that is likely to abrogate and eliminate the old one. The "carry-on spirit" proposed by Averroes as far as the relationship between religion and philosophy is concerned, is likely to be re-invested so as to establish a dialogue between our tradition and universal contemporary thought, a dialogue that would bring us the authenticity and contemporaneity to which we aspire. Averroes preached a religious understanding of a religion that did not draw from beyond the very data of religion, and a philosophical understanding of a philosophy based exclusively on the principles and the intents of philosophy. It is this method that, according to Averroes, was to generate the renewal of both philosophy and religion. Let us again borrow this process from him to identify a way to assume both our relationship to tradition and our relationship to universal contemporary thought, which represents for us what Greek philosophy represented for Averroes. Let us assume our relationship to tradition by understanding it in its proper context, and let us assume our relationship to the universal contemporary thought in the same way. This would enable us to have a scientific and objective understanding of both and would help us invest them jointly along the same perspective: to give a basis to our authenticity within modernity and to give a basis to modernity

within authenticity. Averroes did indeed pose the problem of the relationship to the "Other," which, for us today, is the problem of "contemporaneity" (while to Averroes in the past, the "Other" were the sages of ancient Greece). He approached the problem in a scientific way that should inspire us greatly today. Averroes established a distinction, within the Other's reason, between the instrument it may represent and the subject matter which it constitutes, i.e., between method and theory. He said about the instrument:

(...) it is clear that for our purposes (i.e., the rational study of beings) we must resort to the theses of our precursors in this field, irrespective of whether or not the latter were of our own faith. One does not ask the instrument, e.g., the knife used in the ritual sacrifice whether or not it belonged to one of our fellow Muslims in order to make a judgment on the validity of the sacrifice. One asks of it only to be of suitable use. By those who are not fellow Muslims, we mean those among the ancient ones who had pondered over these questions long before the birth of Islam. Under the circumstances, since all the laws of reasoning (logic and method) have already been perfectly laid down by the ancient ones, we ought to draw from their books by the handful, to find out what they have said about that. If it happens to be correct, we shall welcome it with open arms; if it were to contain something incorrect, we shall make sure to note it.

We must not therefore accept the instrument (the method) as imitators but as careful critics. As for the "subject matter," i.e., the theory, we must construct it by ourselves and for ourselves: "We must undertake the study of the beings according to the order and the manner that the theory of demonstrative syllogisms would teach us," but since it is neither possible nor conceivable to simply repeat the experiences of the predecessors and to rediscover what they discovered before, "[and] when we find among predecessors from the ancient nations a well thought-out conception of the universe—consistent

127

with the conditions required for demonstration—we must examine what they said about it and what they stated in their books. If these things happen to correspond to the truth, we shall gladly welcome them and be grateful to them. If they do not correspond to the truth, we shall make a note of it, warn people against them while excusing their authors..."

Well aware of the universality and historicity of knowledge, Averroes set out to define the way to act when addressing the "the sciences of the ancient ones," which at that time represented science par excellence. This method is worthy of serving as a model. We can reinvest it to define our relationship to tradition and to universal contemporary thought, knowing how to recognize what is universal in both—and that it is possible for us to reinvest in order to re-establish our specificity—and what is particular, what is circumstantial to an era or to a people, which we must know to enrich our experience and our vision of the world.

These are in my opinion the main elements that survive from Averroism, which we can reinvest to address today's problems. I shall summarize them in one phrase: the Averroist spirit. In my call to recover the Averroist spirit, I simply mean this: it must be made present in our thought, in our esteem and in our aspirations in the same way that the Cartesian spirit is present in French thought or that the spirit of empiricism, inaugurated by Locke and by Hume, is present in English thought. Indeed if we were to ask about what is left of Cartesianism in France, or of Locke and Hume's empiricism in England, we would be bound to answer that only one thing has survived in each case. We could refer to it as the Cartesian spirit in France—providing specificity to French thought, or the empiricist spirit in England—providing specificity to English thought. Let us therefore construct our specificity upon what is ours and is particular rather than foreign to us. The Averroist spirit is adaptable to our era because it agrees with it on more than one point: rationalism, realism, axiomatic method and critical approach. To adopt the

Averroist spirit is to break with the Avicennian "oriental" spirit, a gnostic one that promotes *gloom* thinking.

Some Arab intellectuals, who seem to maintain much closer ties with European culture than with the Arab-Islamic tradition, have wondered about how to make Arab thought assimilate the benefits of liberalism "before the Arab world even reaches, let alone undergoes the liberalism phase." Liberalism, for them, is "that school of thought that prevailed in the seventeenth and eighteenth centuries, and by way of which the rising European bourgeoisie fought feudal regimes and ideas." Such is the problematics posed by Abdallah Laroui, Zaki Naguib Mahmoud, Magid Fakhri and others, some following the French and Cartesian point of view, the others following the Anglo-Saxon empiricist and positivist point of view, each according to the type of European "tradition" that represents his own cultural and intellectual frame of reference. We think that it is totally erroneous to pose the problem this way. Because when we ask the Arabs to assimilate European liberalism, we are in effect asking them to incorporate into their consciousness a legacy that is foreign to them with the themes that it raises, the problematics that it poses, and the languages in which it is expressed; a legacy which therefore does not belong in their history. A nation can only bring back to its consciousness a tradition that belongs to it, or something that pertains to that tradition. As for the human legacy in general, with its universal attributes, a nation always experiences it within its own tradition and not outside of it.

I believe that we ought really to set the problematics as follows: how can contemporary Arab thought regain and reinvest the rationalist and the "liberal" gains from its own tradition—in a similar perspective to that within which they were invested the first time: the struggle against feudalism, gnosticism, fatalism, and the will to found a city of reason and justice, to build the free, democratic and socialist Arab city?

This is not a narrowly nationalistic position. We do not in any way want to minimize the great accomplishments of [hu]mankind. We simply think that those accomplishments will always remain foreign to us if we do not invest them following a scientific method that is well-suited to the needs of our historical conditions, in order to solve our own problems. To that end, we must first provide a basis to those great accomplishments within our thought by comparing them to similar accomplishments in our tradition. Here, as elsewhere, our only chance to read our future no longer in the past—or the present—of others, but to construct it from our own reality, from the specificity of our history and the constituents of our personality, is historical consciousness.

---

[1] The parallel established by the author between Al-Farabi's "dream" and Avempace's must be understood as follows: in his Tadbiir *al-mutawahhid* (The Regimen of the Recluse), cf. footnote 28, chapter 5), Avempace had somewhat laid the foundation stone for a philosophical "city" in Al-Andalus, comparable to Al-Farabi's "virtuous city" in the East. But that city belonged to the "solitary" philosopher, as philosophy in his time was both marginalized and persecuted in the Muslim West. It was Averroes who brought it out of isolation and made it emerge to the world, thus founding the city of reason, a reason under whose aegis this world and the hereafter, philosophy and religion, should be placed. Al-Farabi's philosophical city of the East met an opposite fate. Founded for this world, it was replaced by the "illuminist" Avicenna under the aegis of a spiritualism that governed this world as well as the hereafter.